/25   SOC SCI   £7

CW01083676

The Transversal Thought of Gilles Deleuze

The Transversal Thought of Gilles Deleuze: Encounters and Influences

James Williams

Clinamen Press

Copyright © James Williams 2005

First edition published Manchester 2005

Published by Clinamen Press Ltd
Unit B
Aldow Enterprise Park
Blackett Street
Manchester
M12 6AE

www.clinamen.co.uk

All rights reserved. No part of this edition may be reproduced,
stored in or introduced into a retrieval system, or transmitted
in any form or by any means (electronic, mechanical,
photocopying, recording or otherwise) without the written
permission of the publishers

A catalogue record for this book is available from The British Library

ISBN 1 903083 32X

Typeset in Times New Roman

Printed and bound in Great Britain by

Antony Rowe Ltd, Chippenham, Wiltshire

For Heloïse, Olivia and Octie

Contents:

Chapter 5. *Deleuze and Whitehead: the concept of reciprocal determination*

Chapter 6. *Deleuze and Lewis: the real virtual or real possible worlds?*

Chapter 7. *Deleuze and Harman: distinguishing problems from questions*

Chapter 8. *Deleuze, Negri, Lyotard: metaphysics and resistance*

Acknowledgements:

This work was made possible by an AHRB Research Leave Scheme Award in 2003-4. The Carnegie Fund for the Universities Scotland funded further research in Paris libraries in 2004-5. The British Academy funded travel for presentations of versions of the chapters on Kant and on Lewis at the Experimenting with Intensities conference at Trent University, Canada, and at the Australian Society for Continental Philosophy annual conference 2005. I am very grateful for this essential and generous funding. Chapter 5 was presented as part of the "Chromatiques whiteheadiennes" series at the Sorbonne in January 2004. Chapter 7 was given at the Values and Virtues conference in Dundee, May 2004. The final chapter on resistance was presented at the Society for European Philosophy annual conference, University of Greenwich, July 2004. Chapter 4 was presented at the Gaston Bachelard: The History of Society conference at Goldsmiths College, University of London, in December 2003. Chapter 2 was presented at Carleton University, Ottawa, in May 2004. Chapter 6 was presented in part at the 'Que prouve la science-fiction: raison, machines, corps et mondes' conference, Université de Lille 3, 1-2 April 2005. The chapter on Deleuze and Kant was presented, in a different version, at the Experimenting with Intensities conference in May 2004. Questions, criticisms and suggestions put to me at all these occasions were invaluable in improving this work and I am grateful to all participants - but reserve all errors as mine! Many friends, postgraduate students and colleagues helped with support and ideas. I thank them all and, in particular, for remedying lack of knowledge and oversight, or for helpful suggestions: Isabella Palin, Lars Iyer, Keith Robinson, Rachel Jones, Michel Weber, Will Large, John Protevi, Nicholas Davey, John Mullarkey, Keith Ansell Pearson, Paul Barlow, Fabio Presutti, Tim Flanagan, Jenny Kermally and William Ross. Without the love of Claire, Rebecca, Nathan and Alice, this book would never have been written.

1

Introduction:
the problem of openness
in metaphysics

'The construction of the most open, far-reaching and well-determined metaphysics.' This book develops an interpretation of Gilles Deleuze's work around the problem drawn up by this phrase. The interpretation is but one of the multiple ways Deleuze's work can be taken up and read. It neither aims to be comprehensive, nor faithful - in that rather sad and unreflective sense of 'true to' as devotedly close to the words or spirit of a master or of masterworks. Instead, a series of tensions and contradictions that define the problem will guide discussions of relations between Deleuze and six other philosophers (Kant, Bachelard, Whitehead, Levinas, Lewis and Harman). The restricted terms of the discussions should not be taken as signs of irrelevance at the level of the problem. Quite the contrary: the problem reverberates throughout Deleuze's many works and contributions. Where these impact on life, so does the problem, with its tensions and difficulties, but also with its productive power.

Since the problem and its conditions are bare and brute, the choice of thinkers is not so much arbitrary as tendentious. Other encounters and influences could have been selected, perhaps with more felicitous outcomes, perhaps not. These are my selections. They are made against a background of philosophical, academic and political motivations, some of which define a small world of academic training and competition, others much wider social and philosophical problems, others, the simple limitations of a brain, a body and the surroundings - near and far - that work on them over a stretch of time. Nonetheless, in charting a way through the twin pressures of how to maximally diminish the restraining and exclusive tendencies of metaphysics, whilst also creating structures that interact in an enriching and deepening manner with others, the selection seemed the one best suited to each of the main threats to a successful response to the original metaphysical problem.

This focus on problems and their internal tensions explains the decisions not to include certain major influences (Nietzsche and Bergson, for example) and encounters (Heidegger, Derrida and Foucault, to cite some of the major omissions). Whilst each of these will be or has been the subject of important work on Deleuze, their meetings with him seemed to take the question of metaphysics towards problems that I was not attracted to, or capable of covering in depth. In many cases, others have already done so, much better than I could or than my focus would allow.[1] A gesture towards the reasons for selection, or at least the ones that I am conscious of, could be that this book rests on the premises that there is a Deleuzian metaphysics, that it plays an important and irreplaceable role in his philosophy, and that it raises significant but not fatal problems.[2]

But what do 'open', 'determined' and 'metaphysics' mean in the context of Deleuze's work? Here, a metaphysics is taken to be a dynamic structure of relations between philosophical concepts and ideas. It is the productive heart of a philosophical system, not understood as the most important basic forms, but as the interaction of the most productive and original ones, with one another, but also with more distant and secondary orders. A metaphysics is therefore not a separate order or set of concepts and ideas. Nor is it a worldview, or a simplified representation of life, or a philosophical response to physical theories. It is rather the genetic core of a philosophical system in its ongoing transformative relation to the worlds it draws up and that, in return, feed into it (whether these worlds be actual, virtual, possible or real - or, as we shall see, all four).

For example, were a philosophy to be constructed around two substances (mind and body, say), the idea of metaphysics used here would lead to studies of the relations between these terms and of their wider repercussions. Judgments that the world could be divided into mind and body, or that truth could be defined in terms of one but not the other, or that one was superior to the other, would be less important than the way mind and body interacted and how that relation led to series of further dynamic effects. Questions of openness would enter in terms of which relations and what kinds of relations were not allowed by the philosophy, of which relations operated in setting up the core ones, and which transformed them.

This is not to say that any metaphysics could exhaust or capture, represent or condense, direct or control the wider worlds or world that it interacts with. The relations are much more complex and multi-directional. Different pressures accompany different-scaled effects and affections across systems with no key or chart to finally decide on importance and on priorities. A flash of inspiration in only one body at a particular time can run through a philosophical system, just as it does through a set of literary works or a life. Equally, though, an idea, sometime a vile and terrible idea, can have strong metaphysical roots and go on to poison minds, bodies and societies, driving them to terrible destruction.

Yet, one of the claims here is that metaphysics matters because, as a genetic core in process, it is to be distinguished from other structures within a system of worlds and lives. The distinguishing features of a metaphysics are its consistency, economy and reach. The elements of the metaphysical structure are very tightly related (perhaps logically, but also through many other forms of internal relations; semantically, for example). It may not even be possible to separate the elements and retain their sense. A principle of economy runs alongside this consistency. There can be no inoperative idea or redundant concept, nor unproductive or uninteresting contradiction or paradox. Finally, metaphysical structures are disproportionately powerful. They resonate through other structures to an extent and with a transformative power that is unmatched by others, both in terms of manner and of effect.

So, though the genetic core can make no claim to independence, since it is related to other structures that transform it and its effects, it can make claims to greater consistency and power. Yet power, here, must not be understood in its everyday sense of a capacity to change others at will or at least to hold that capacity in suspense in such a way that it can be released reliably and relatively predictably. Metaphysical structures have their own scales and essences in terms of time and space, that is, they determine time and space, not directly in the physical sense, but in the sense of our understanding and ideas about that physical sense. This determination is deeply unreliable both in terms of time (metaphysical reach can lie latent for centuries) and in terms of value judgements about spatial effects (insignificant distinctions can turn out to be crucial, dependent on when and where they come into play; innocent and neutral ideas can turn out to be some of the most violent, whilst scandalous ones can set off the most liberating waves).

This statement against metaphysical independence is one of the most tendentious of this book, since it sets up a predisposition against a series of positions very distant from Deleuze's. It is important, therefore, to see my definition of metaphysics as a speculative move. Many of the discussions to follow problematise the claim to metaphysical relativity and complexity, for example, through challenges to the important Deleuzian concept of continuity. If those challenges are judged to be successful, then a different definition of metaphysics will have to follow. Indeed, one of the most characteristic aspects of any metaphysics is that it carries its own definition of its form and purpose within it. This is due to the demands for consistency and economy. A metaphysics does not overtly rest on something external to it, without determining that relation on its own terms, not fully, but necessarily. This is not to say that there aren't external relations. It is to say that, when these relations are made overt, the metaphysics must rise to new and often difficult stresses.

Equally, the very focus on metaphysics should be treated with great suspicion, since it jumps ahead of a series of possible interpretations of Deleuze and also invites a series of serious criticisms that interpretations avoiding metaphysical moves can claim to sidestep. Here, too, each discussion raises the danger of metaphysical moves in philosophy as well as suggesting counters. However, the possible claim that Deleuze's work is completely devoid of such moves is not addressed directly. Indirectly, though, each of the following chapters attempts to show the search for consistency, economy and reach in Deleuze's connection of ideas and concepts through philosophical methods and arguments. The subtext is that it is simply implausible to view him as a naïve positivist or materialist - a position akin in its absurdity to viewing him as a religious thinker.

I define openness in metaphysics as a relation that does not impose restrictions on future transformations and events. A metaphysics that sets down the path of the world from now to some final judgement day, or a metaphysics indebted to a particular science or set of laws, or one that sets out fundamental ontological forms and elements would not be open. Each of these restrictions drives different aspects of Deleuze's philosophy: from the desire to avoid forms of religious transcendence (Deleuze's debt to Spinoza); to the lessons learnt from mistaken commitments to transient sciences - or at least to their transient exclusivity or pre-eminence - (Deleuze's debt to Hume); up to the drive to unmask the external processes and connections at work within any supposedly fundamental identity (his debt to Nietzsche).

Yet, one of the reasons Deleuze can take his place within the long but sparse line of these great thinkers is that he takes this commitment to openness further than any other - perhaps because he follows a narrowing spiral of different attempts to achieve it. A contention of the interpretation set out here is that openness can be seen as a key to unlock the connectedness, economy and reach of Deleuze's metaphysics. His work is an attempt to construct a system that unfolds productively and openly, yet free from, or at least relatively resistant to, the return to any belief in eternal transcendent forms (principally religious or traceable to religious instincts and consequences), fixed scientific forms (laws, explanations, practices and methods), restricting philosophical methodological forms (representation, recognition and negation) and closed ontological forms (essences, properties, individuals, species, kinds).

This demand for openness explains the definition of metaphysics as a dynamic structure. It would be uninterestingly contradictory to have a fixed set of distinctions, objects or beings at the core of a metaphysics claiming openness. Instead, Deleuze's metaphysics must be seen as essentially about process and about transforming relations. As such, the genetic structure is one that sets others in movement and draws up principles for guarding against the return to fixity in itself and in the most far-flung worlds and ideas. The reach of Deleuze's metaphysics is movement. Its genetic role is to transfer movement from and to other structures, where movement must not be understood as mechanical, in the sense of a simple displacement of elements, but as evolutionary, in the sense of a transformation of those elements beyond what they have become settled in. This evolution cannot posit the independence or even primacy of the genetic core as a set of fixed elements or structures. Instead, extended relations are primary and a problem is first and foremost a matter of the creative and destructive strains and releases that run through complete structures of relations.

Thus, when taken with the demand to maximize them, openness and reach are self-defeating terms. They also serve to cancel each other out. This is the most striking aspect of the problem of metaphysics under consideration here. If a structure is to be open, both internally and in the way it drives openness in others, it appears to be destined to lose its own identity, to the point where a capacity to discriminate becomes lost. This inability can be taken as a model for the problem. It emerges out of the difficulty of balancing an avoidance of 'discrimination', in its negative sense of an unjust treatment of others because they fall outside a privileged identity, with an inability to 'discriminate', in its positive sense of a capacity to introduce distinctions. Openness is therefore caught between chaos and exclusion, both of which defeat the demand to invite difference without prejudging it. In its openness to everything, chaos is open to nothing. In exclusion, there is no openness - worse, there are the seeds for further exclusions and injustices.

A similar problem is caused by reach. In order to reach far, a core structure must dilute its identity within that with which it interacts, or it must impose its identity at a distance. In both cases, there is no real reach, since an overstretching is nothing but a loss, either as the incorporation into a distant identity or in a more generalized and once again chaotic loss of any determinacy. To inflict an identity upon another is no reach at all. It is merely to eliminate what is strange, different and disturbing, to the point where the productive value of each side is lost and where the ethical interaction between individuals is denied in favour of an imposition. There is then only the illusion of reach, when in fact a structure has stood still, all the better to cancel out others. Yet, when reach is defined as making connections with different structures and openness is defined, narrowly, as the search for as minimal an identity as possible, the two become contradictory. If an open structure is one that imposes as few restrictions on what can occur as possible, by seeking as little identity as possible, it appears to be incapable of carrying the richness and determinacy required to interact positively with other structures. It is as if we were caught between the still only relatively open option of speaking a given set of languages, and thereby carrying the danger of defining language exclusively in terms of this set, or of speaking none, and thereby failing to interact with others whilst not imposing on their possibility.

In response to these contradictions, Deleuze's metaphysics seeks determinacy whilst maintaining openness. This means to avoid chaos or an obligation to otherness that blocks any substantial interaction, and yet, also, to avoid identity. The challenge is then to determine a metaphysical structure as a process that neither restricts new events, nor sets down an internal set of fixed elements. To do this, Deleuze defines his structure as one of transform- ing relations, rather than of primary relations between identities. His structure is one that undermines identities, but that therefore also gives them place and function, if not a fundamental one.

His metaphysical strategy is to define inter-related realms that cannot be considered complete without one another. These realms depend on each other for their determinacy, that is, for the relative determinacy of terms within them in relation to others, in the way some relations stand out from others against an infinite receding background constituted by others. To use a key term from Deleuze: they are in a relation of reciprocal determination. This relation cannot be unraveled back to a first origin, be subjected to an external logic that gives it a set direction and order, or traced to a final end. The kind of determinacy afforded by these relations varies according to what is deter- mined.

One realm, the actual, allows for relative and transient identities, whilst the other, the virtual, allows for all the transforming processes that sunder those identities. This chaotic 'all' of processes acquires determinacy in the way it is set to work on actual identities. A restricted set of actual identities, set down in a given and illusory account of what we know, is given determinacy through its relation to all virtual processes and how it gives them determinacy. So to be determined takes on a special sense for Deleuze. It is to be complete, though not whole, in the sense of related to all processes in an individual way.

An individual is a series of identities set in movement in a singular way by a series of virtual processes. Thereby, any individual is connected to all other individuals and their singularities and sundered identities, because their singularity is only a distinctness in relation to every other virtual relation and identity. An individual is the whole of the world under a singular perspective, which must not be understood as a single and all-encompassing vision, but as a singular distinctness of processes. This connectedness and completeness explain the great reach of Deleuze's metaphysics. The relations of identity to prior transforming processes are its openness. No identity, no method for accounting for identity is in principle untouchable, because no identity is untouched. Yet both openness and reach are achieved through a complex account of processes that does not leave forms loosely or minimally determined; quite the contrary, each individual must be approached according to principles that demand its complete determination as actual, virtual, singular, and in its interference with other individuals.

Each of the following chapters explains Deleuze's metaphysics and the problem of openness in detail. The focus of each chapter is on a particular problem defined in terms of a particular encounter, though, like the metaphysics, these are all interlinked and treat related difficulties to different degrees of depth. The chapter on Deleuze and Kant addresses the problem of how to work in transcendental philosophy, but without returning to forms of transcendence. The chapter on Deleuze and Levinas considers the ethical consequences of Deleuze's philosophy in terms of different ways of understanding expression and the role of the face in ethics; it asks whether Deleuze's metaphysics is genuinely open in terms of ethical relations to others. The chapter on Bachelard addresses the problem of negation in metaphysics, in particular in terms of Bachelard's claims to its necessity and in terms of how to define dialectics in order to retain openness in metaphysics. In the encounter between Deleuze and Whitehead, the focus is on problems of metaphysical dualism and the ways in which different definitions of reciprocal determination commit to prior identities, at the expense of openness with respect to relations. The chapter on Deleuze and Lewis assesses the different merits of appeals to the possible and to the virtual in metaphysics. It looks in detail at an opposition between two ways of appealing to pragmatism in relation alternately to creativity and to common sense. This is then followed up, in the chapter on Deleuze and Harman, with a critique of analytic moral philosophy and its relation to common sense. This chapter also raises and answers the criticism of Deleuze that his philosophy is either impossibly abstract or impossibly complex and that, therefore, it is not genuinely open at all when compared to recent developments in analytic moral philosophy. The last chapter raises the problem of where to situate resistance in Deleuze's metaphysics from the point of view of difficulties raised by Negri and answers suggested by Lyotard.

Notes

1) For example, for the encounter with Derrida see Paul Patton and John Protevi (eds.) *Between Deleuze and Derrida* (London: Continuum, 2004). For the encounter with Heidegger, see Miguel de Beistegui's *Truth and Genesis: Philosophy as Differential Ontology* (Indiana University Press: 2004). For the encounter with Bergson see *Philosophy and the Adventure of the Virtual: Bergson and the Philosophy of Time* (London: Routledge, 2002) esp. Chapter 4. For a much broader discussion of Deleuze's relation to Whitehead see Isabelle Stengers *Penser avec Whitehead: une libre et sauvage creation de concepts* (Paris: Seuil, 2002). For the encounter with phenomenology and Merleau-Ponty in particular, see Dorothea Olkowski *Gilles Deleuze and the Ruin of Representation* (University of California Press, 1999). For inevitably and understandably partisan accounts of the encounters with Badiou and Zizek see, respectively, their own *Deleuze: "la clameur de l'être"* (Paris: Hachette, 1997) and *Organs without Bodies: Deleuze and Consequences* (London: Routledge, 2003). For encounters with historical figures generally see Michael Hardt's *Gilles Deleuze: an Apprenticeship in Philosophy* (University of Minnesota Press, 1993) and, for Spinoza, and perhaps more critically than the arguments put forward here, Gillian Howie *Deleuze and Spinoza: Aura of Expressionism* (Basingstoke: Palgrave, 2002). Of course, nothing should come before the pleasure of reading Deleuze's own works on the history of philosophy.

2) Much of the systematic work underpinning this turn to metaphysics and to specific problems was developed in my commentary on Deleuze's *Difference and Repetition, Gilles Deleuze's Difference and Repetition: A Critical Introduction and Guide* (Edinburgh University Press, 2003)

8

2

Deleuze and Kant:
the transcendental
without transcendence

The reader must therefore be convinced of the unavoidable necessity of such a transcendental deduction before he has taken a single step in the field of pure reason. Otherwise he proceeds blindly, and after manifold wanderings must come back to the same ignorance from which he started. At the same time, if he is not to lament over obscurity in matters which are by their very nature deeply veiled, or to be too easily discouraged in the removal of these obstacles, he must have a clear foreknowledge of the inevitable difficulty of the undertaking. (*Immanuel Kant*, Critique of Pure Reason, 123)

Far from deriving from the present or from representation, the past is presupposed by any representation. It is in this sense that, though the active synthesis of memory may well be founded on the (empirical) passive synthesis of habit, it must be founded by another (transcendental) passive synthesis proper to memory itself. Whilst the passive synthesis of habit constitutes the living present in time, and makes of past and future the two asymmetrical elements of that present, the passive synthesis of memory constitutes the pure past in time, and makes the old present and the actual (thus the present in reproduction and the future in reflection) the two asymmetrical elements of that past as such. (*Gilles Deleuze*, Difference and Repetition, 81, 110)

Deleuze's debt to Kant

Deleuze's debt to Kant is played out through differences between prepositions as they apply to synthesis and to the transcendental. The prepositions are 'on', 'by', 'of', 'to' and 'in'. Deleuze wants to adopt Kant's work on transcendental deductions and on synthesis. He wants to emphasise the power of that work to move synthesis away from a direct grounding, where things rest on it, to an indirect conditioning 'by' the transcendental condition 'of' the given. He also argues that Kant diminishes that power, by still referring the transcendental 'to' a form of transcendence, when in fact all things should be thought of as 'in' the transcendental. For Deleuze, though rich in resources, Kant's critical philosophy is still one of transcendence rather than immanence.

In *Difference and Repetition*, synthesis can be asymmetrical or symmetrical. In the latter instance, the one that concerns us most here, the result of the synthesis is different from the things that are synthesised and the process of synthesis cannot be reversed. The synthesis can also be passive or active. It is active as the direct result of the actions of a subject - of its identifications and representations. It is passive when repetitions, beyond the grasp of identity and representation, come to form new syntheses. There is a key opposition, in Deleuze, between the conscious association of a subject with an identity and a goal and the unconscious association of differing movements into looser or tighter sets of relations.

Passive synthesis itself allows for at least two different senses. Things, for example memory, can be *founded on* a passive synthesis - made by it. But that process can itself be *founded by* another passive synthesis that stands as its condition, rather than as its maker or cause. So, in the passage quoted in exergue, when Deleuze describes two different passive syntheses, one of memory and one of habit, what matters is how that synthesis functions: 'founded on' (through repetition) or 'founded by' (as a condition).

In the first case, the content of a thing - its predicates, or identifiable components - can be traced back directly to external causes. For example, in tracing a particular physical characteristic back to a particular genetic mutation. In the second, a distinction must be drawn between Kant and Deleuze. For the former, abstracted universal forms are seen to presuppose pure transcendental forms. For the latter, singular events in sensibility are seen to presuppose pure transcendental forms.

Kant's critical philosophy bequeaths transcendental deductions to Deleuze's work, but in very different guises and contexts. Deleuze's transcendental work allows him to deduce the necessary reciprocal determination of the actual and the virtual through transcendental deductions. For Kant, in such deductions, a priori conditions are deduced as necessary for the general forms of objects and for their universal synthesis.

The crux of the matter, here, lies in the consequences of presupposition

(Why does it matter that something is presupposed?) and in the arguments for necessity (How do we know that this presupposition is necessary?). Deleuze's early book on Kant, *Kant's Critical Philosophy*, focuses on both questions in its treatment of Kant's work on the transcendental.

Deleuze connects the two problems through the question of why phenomena should be subjected to the legislation of the understanding. In other words, why should pure a priori forms (Kant's categories) allow for judging what the necessary form should be for any empirical presentation:

> Phenomena are not subject to the synthesis of the imagination; they are subjected by this synthesis to the legislative understanding. Unlike space and time, the categories as concepts of the understanding are thus made the object of a transcendental deduction, which poses and resolves the special problems of a subjection of phenomena. (17)

Deleuze's answer is that all phenomena must appear in space and time. Space and time must themselves be synthesised in the imagination prior to any experience. The transcendental conditions for this synthesis, the unity of space and time and the categories must therefore hold for all phenomena.

It is important, at this stage, to avoid a confusion between two uses of the term 'pure form'. This distinction follows the difference between the *analysis* of the unity of space and time, which gives us pure a priori forms (the categories) and the *abstraction* from particular phenomena to their general pure form (how all phenomena must appear in space and time). The deduction submits general pure forms to the demands of pure a priori forms - phenomena to categories.

Thus, conditions that are independent of all experience are deduced as having to hold for there to be any possible object in appearance and for there to be a synthetic unity of thought about such objects (*Critique of Pure Reason*, 120-5). Transcendental philosophy therefore has a functional sense, that is, the deduction shows that a priori conditions hold for empirical objects. 'To hold' means to validly fulfill the function of legislating. 'Legislating' means judging the legitimacy of a case before a given faculty; for the understanding, it is to judge whether a proposition can count as knowledge about an object, that is, whether it is consistent with the categories.

The most important aspect of these deductions lies in the a priori, since it would be impossible to deduce necessary conditions for general forms empirically, as shown by Hume's work on induction - to which Kant is responding explicitly through the conceptual innovation of transcendental deductions (CPR, 127):

11

> Appearances do indeed present cases from which a rule can be obtained according to which something usually happens, but they never prove the sequence to be necessary... This strict universality of the rule is never a characteristic of empirical rules; they can acquire through induction only comparative universality, that is, extensive applicability. (CPR 125)

Deleuze is particularly concerned with this resistance to Hume and to crude empiricism. He uses it to frame the discussion of the transcendental in *Kant's Critical Philosophy* (see also 'Hume' and 'L'Idée de genèse dans l'esthétique de Kant').[3] I shall argue that he depends on it for his own resistance to empiricism and deduction of a different kind of transcendental necessity in *Difference and Repetition*.

However, the great difficulty with Deleuze's relation to Kant lies in the fact that Deleuze does not adopt deductions and the transcendental without profoundly transforming the terms and without developing a strong set of critical remarks on Kant's version. So Deleuze's debt to Kant is ambiguous - as it is to almost all the great figures touched on through *Difference and Repetition*. The encounter with Kant is of the order of a clash of two systems with the highest claims to internal consistency. Deleuze's adoption of transcendental deductions is then also a diversion. The key question must be whether it is a misappropriation or a valuable rerouting.

Some parameters of this question are internal to Deleuze's engagement with Kant. Are the points of departure from Kant legitimate refinements, or do they invalidate his methods? Is Deleuze's departure logically consistent and valid with respect to its main arguments? Do they allow for a continuity from one thinker to the other? Or are there radical differences that stage profound ethical and political divergences?

Other parameters are external. Is it possible to identify Deleuze's debt to Kant with any accuracy, or must we be resigned to finding a complex hotchpotch of many debts, where the identification of any particular strain becomes a false simplification? For example, can Bergson's work on memory be sifted out of the passage quoted in exergue, to leave a pure Kantian legacy?

Forms and foundations

All the above questions will be touched on here. But priority will be given to a particular pair of problems. Why does Deleuze need to appeal to Kant at some of the most brittle points of his arguments? Is that appeal successful? Deleuze depends on Kantian transcendental deductions to justify his claim that reality is a complex structure of relations between, on the one hand, virtual Ideas and intensities and, on the other, actual sensations, intensities again, and identifications. But this dependency itself relies on a far reaching transformation of Kant's method that leads to severe critical arguments against Kant and equally difficult questions regarding the validity of Deleuze's project.

The passage quoted in exergue exhibits many of these problems. It is from Deleuze's deduction of the second synthesis of time from chapter II of *Difference and Repetition*. It occurs just before his discussion of Bergson's arguments for the pure past in *Matter and Memory*, and just after a series of questions designed to show that the actual cannot only be referred to a first synthesis of time defined as habit.

In order to extend his treatment of time to a second synthesis, Deleuze has moved from a first sensation in the 'living present' (*present vivant*), the sensation of expectation or forward momentum through the present, to a second sensation, of passing away in the present into archive, into the past. He is not concerned to make a clear-cut distinction between these sensations and the syntheses of time. On the contrary, the point is to show their interdependence.

This structural dependence draws out Deleuze's profound reliance on Kant and the importance of the vocabulary highlighted above. The specific passage links a discussion of a Humean treatment of synthesis as habit to a Bergsonian treatment of synthesis as the underlying synthesis of the pure past with each passing present.

However, a much larger undertaking is also at stake: the construction of a transcendental structure of asymmetrical relations of reciprocal determination ('It is in this sense that, though the active synthesis of memory may well be founded on the (empirical) passive synthesis of habit, it must be founded by another (transcendental) passive synthesis proper to memory itself'). It is here that Kant's influence is all-important.

This explains why Deleuze stresses relations of founding (the founding of active memory on habit and by a transcendental passive synthesis). What he means is that there are two conditions for acts of memory. The first is not transcendental, it is the way repetitions empirically lead to a form of action; that is, we only learn how to remember by repeating the many different acts that compose active memory. This empirical synthesis can be understood as practice. It is a form of condition associated with particular acts and that can be generalised as a condition for any particular act of memory. Active memory only becomes determined through the repetitions of habit. This is the founding *of* something.

In contrast, the second condition explains what active memories must be conditioned by, not for the determining of their content, but for the determining of their form. This form is not proper to active memory alone, but to any act accompanied by a sense of passing away in the living present. As we experience an act of memory we also experience it as a passing away into something that itself can be remembered. Here, Deleuze is not asking how a particular act came to be, but what the condition is for a sense of passing away as a form of the living present. This is where Deleuze rejoins Kant's work on the transcendental; it is where a sensation is founded *by* a transcendental a priori condition.

Transcendental condition and 'founded by' therefore have a positive source as that which is presupposed by the form of something, in terms of what explains its determinacy. They also have a negative source, in the sense of an opposition to causal empirical processes. This means that the transcendental condition cannot be of the same kind as that which it determines, or cannot belong to the same realm - hence the insistence on asymmetrical synthesis.

Condition and conditioned are radically different. Deleuze will say 'heterogeneous'. When the transcendental condition founds a different realm - in this case the realm of the actual or living present - the two realms are 'asymmetrical', that is, the laws or processes that relate things in one realm are not those that relate things in the other. In fact, this implies that the elements of each realm must be different since they are constituted by those laws or processes.

But Deleuze takes the relation of condition and conditioned much further than Kant, since he still wants to hold to a process-like or quasi-causal relation between them. This is what he means by the reciprocal determination of the virtual and the actual: the virtual founds the actual and the actual founds the virtual, that is, the transcendental condition is itself determined by the actual.

There is an opposition between two senses of condition here. Kant seeks the a priori conditions for a pure general form appearing in the synthesis of space and time, for example, for what pure intuition presupposes as the mere form of appearances (CPR 67). The condition is presupposed by the general form and hence by any empirical given as it appears according to that pure form (intuition, reason or judgement, for instance). This means that the condition does not vary or depend upon differences between empirical cases of the same kind, neither should it reflect inconsistencies or variations in them. The pure form is abstract and invariant, so is its condition.

Whereas, in the Deleuzian sense of transcendental deduction, there is no pure general form, where this form is understood as a purification of things that resemble one another and that are the same in what they share with the pure form. Instead, the form is a sensibility that accompanies actual situations and identifications. So there is not a pure general form of phenomena, there is a sensation detachable from the identities that it occurs with. A priori forms will be deduced for that sensation.

This distinction is very important, since, firstly, the sensation is contingent and singular in Deleuze. It is not pure and its claim to generality is not as the necessary form for any phenomenon. Instead, its claim to extend beyond the singular is through an expression or communication based on a dramatisation. Deleuze tries to express the way in which certain sensations accompany things like memory or actions, but the force of his arguments depends on making us feel that he is right. They are contingent on our sensations in response to his dramatisation (for an excellent discussion of dramatisation with respect to reciprocal determination, see Deleuze's 'La méthode de dramatisation' esp. pp 139-40).

Secondly, sensations are defined as resistant to conceptual identification. This explains the need for dramatisation, since sensations are required for the transmission or expression of sensations - no communication of a concept would suffice. Therefore, in opposition to Kant's need to deduce the presuppositions of the synthesis of space and time in a pure and invariant general form, Deleuze has to deduce the presuppositions of the resistance to identification in an open set of variations.

The form of the condition cannot be fixed in such a way as to deny the variability of the different sensations it founds. The condition must vary with them, not only as singular sensations, but between different sensations. The given is an open set of variations, each of which denies identity - including identity in the pure form. Thus each given sensation implies a way of differentiating transcendental conditions. How to account for this difference, whilst resisting atomism or an indeterminate chaos is the greatest challenge of Deleuzian metaphysics. It is also the source of much of its metaphysical creativity, notably, in terms of virtual intensities and Ideas, defined as multiplicities of relations between non-identifiable variations.

For Kant, there can be no transforming relation between the given and its condition. Instead, the relation is an invariant asymmetrical one: the a priori necessary condition follows necessarily from the pure form. Empirical a posteriori cases of the form are regulated by the condition for which it stands as a necessary law (for example, there cannot be knowledge of an object that defies the category of causality).

Here, 'regulation' means that the condition provides the laws that govern any possible true statement about those cases, not insofar as they can be

15

thought of as manifestations of 'things in themselves' but as things that must conform to the pure a priori form.

For Deleuze, there must be a transforming relation so as not to fix the given in their internal variations, that is, the a priori form must be sufficiently open to vary according to different empirical events. The relation must be between varying and open conditions: new sensations must not be eliminated a priori, nor must actual variation in any given sensation.

It could be claimed that Kant also allows for variation insofar as empirical objects vary but leave the pure form unaffected (somewhat like the way we can have many different particular individuals conforming to the same kind). But this variation is still limited by the form and this is what Deleuze cannot allow for, since he does not want to impose limits on the variation described. It cannot admit a pure form.

This could lead to a criticism of Deleuze in terms of the possibility of giving any accurate description of a given. Does this not have to presuppose some kind of limitation and form? The answer is yes, but that this is an incomplete and contingent limitation. We have to identify something, but our experience of it always exceeds that identification. Deleuze's deductions do not begin with phenomena identified under concepts, they begin with intense experiences of variation outside the boundaries of identifications.

So the relation he describes is a varying asymmetrical one: the condition is determined in different ways by each given and each given is justified as varying and resistant to identification by the condition. Here, 'determined' means given its singularity as something that stands out from either an indeterminate multiplicity of variations (for the condition), or from a set series of identities, in the case of the given.

This distinction allows us to return to the guiding questions on Deleuze's debt to Kant. How far can Deleuze's redefinition of the transcendental away from the a priori and from pure forms be sustained, since it seems to commit him to contingent beginnings which belie the universality sought by Kant? How far can Deleuze's insistence on the reciprocal determination of condition and conditioned be maintained in the face of the objection that this quasi-causality is a fictional distortion of scientific causal regularity?

In other words, since Deleuze is committed to a contingent transcendental, is he open to the objection that the real conditions for such empirical forms must be sought in empirical causes and not in abstract transcendental ones? The key questions then become: 'What arguments does Deleuze have for the validity of transcendental deductions that are not based on pure beginnings? How does he avoid the accusation that he is replacing Kant's legitimating conditions with quasi-causal ones (and hence quasi-mystical or downright contradictory ones)?

Immanence and the transcendental

Deleuze describes reality as the reciprocal relations holding between a transcendental realm of virtual Ideas and intensities and a realm of actual sensations and identifications. Virtual Ideas are multiplicities of pure variations, resistant to representation and conceptualisation, but dependent on processes of actualisation for their complete determination. A process of actualisation is where virtual Ideas and intensities are expressed through actual things. Intensities are the virtual conditions for the emergence of actual sensations and for the determination of Ideas.

It is important to resist any identification of Deleuze's Ideas with ideas commonly understood as representations in the mind. For him, an Idea is a multiplicity of variations, a complex of varying intensities that can only be understood as something like actual ideas, the idea of a revolution, say, at the cost of imposing a restrictive image on the pure Idea. Were Ideas like ideas in the mind, then Deleuze's claim that they were virtual and conditions for the actual would collapse.

Though intensities are resistant to all forms of measure and comparison, they determine variations in Ideas and sensations through their reconfigurations or 'perplications'. That is, intensities fold over one another and thereby cover or reveal each other. In this way they exacerbate or dim their roles within Ideas and sensations, but without changing in themselves. Sensations are disruptions within actual identifications, they are signs of the expression of Ideas and intensities in actual structures.

There is no denying the difficulty of Deleuze's account of reality - necessary for an understanding of the role played by Kantian arguments. It may therefore be helpful to think in terms of an example. You have waited years to see a loved one again, tarrying with dimming memories and shifts in longings and needs. A meeting has been arranged. The opening gestures, words and images bring together fixed memories and preconceptions (actual identifications) with feelings that destroy them (actual sensations of disappointment, excitement, bemusement, renewed passion).

The power of these sensations cannot come solely from the disrupted identities, rather, they are expressions of deeper charges (virtual intensities). But, beyond local identifications and their more and more distant actual effects, imagined and even undreamed worlds of Ideas are changed through the meeting.

According to Deleuze, these are not possible worlds, but virtual ones

17

that ground actual identifications. The actual meeting is accompanied by a virtual one, where Ideas take shape and acquire significance through shifts in relations between intensities. These shifts light up actual situations in new ways and determine different Ideas to come into play.

The meeting is a failure. Intensities push feelings of disappointment to the fore, destroying one world of Ideas and perhaps determining a colder one with greater clarity. The meeting is a success. Feelings of anticipation and excitement come to express the dominance of intensities associated with Ideas of hope and growth. In truth, for Deleuze, the meeting is always a matter of degrees of success *and* failure - they only differ through the varying lighting of intensities. Ideas only become more obscure or brighter as their relations to one another shift. They never leave the scene altogether.

For Deleuze, life is like a structure of identifiable shapes and concepts, given significance by the sensations, intensities and Ideas that flow through and determine individuals. These sensations allow us to follow trails of values through what would ordinarily be cold and neutral spaces. The genesis of sensations cannot come from the spaces themselves, instead, they depend on shifts in intensities associated with all the Ideas that press themselves on individuals in their relations to neutral spaces.

Think of life as a meeting of sensations, Ideas and actual identifiable functions. When you stand in muted frustration before a bureaucratic dead-end, life is the whole situation, covering Ideas, feelings and actual processes. The actual bureaucracy makes perfect rational sense to itself and to many others who use it daily without hindrance. For you, it triggers sensations that come from somewhere far removed from this apparent rationality (the virtual realm of intensities and Ideas). According to Deleuze, there is no self-sufficient cold actuality - it always depends on the lighting of intensities through sensations to acquire significance and to evolve.

Or, to use an analogy, it is as if the actual were a structure of pencil lines, lacking colour (intensity) to make it fully significant for us. That colour is fundamentally different from the lines and infuses them according to different principles than those that govern the lines (perspective, for example). The condition for these principles lies in a realm completely free of lines (the virtual) where colours and their chaotic relations are given passing determinacy through their association in Ideas that relate the colours to particular actual cases of their application. The Idea of the pastoral idyll relates intensities of colours and actual sensations of a pastoral scene - different painters determine different Ideas and different actual scenes.

In the move from the actual to the virtual, sensations relate flows of intensities to events at the level of unconscious Ideas. Actual threats, injustices, cruelty, stupidity, but also needs, loves and delights are accompanied by intense sensations. These sensations are expressions of a virtual life that flows through the actual one. Each one of 'us' (like each painter, above) has individual sensations that explain our irreducible difference from others. Each one of us is an expression of a virtual life from an individual angle: 'A life is everywhere, in all the moments a certain living subject passes through and that certain lived objects regulate: immanent life carrying along the events or singularities which do nothing more than actualise themselves in subjects and objects.' ('Immanence: a life' 172)

In this passage from Deleuze's last article, written nearly 30 years after *Difference and Repetition*, he is once again drawing our attention to the virtual world of intensities and ideal events that give value to identifiable subjects and objects. An individual is partly this process of actualisation, where the virtual bursts into the actual: 'What we call virtual is not something that lacks reality, but something that enters into a process of actualisation by following the plane that gives it its own reality.' (IAL, 173)

More importantly for the encounter between Kant and Deleuze, 'Immanence: a life…' explicitly links the virtual to the idea of a transcendental field. In so doing, Deleuze also makes a significant criticism of Kant's work on the transcendental:

> When the subject and the object, being outside the plane of immanence, are taken as universal subject or object in general *to* which immanence is itself attributed, then the transcendental is completely denatured and merely reduplicates the empirical (as in Kant) while immanence is deformed and ends up being contained in the transcendent.(IAL, 171)

In this return to Kant and to prepositions in relation to the transcendental, Deleuze's concern is two-fold. First, he wants to ensure that the transcendental is not subordinated to something that lies outside it and that runs counter to it. This is why he negatively highlights the preposition 'to'. The transcendental, defined as a field of immanence, must always be thought of, in terms of relations, as qualified by an 'in', rather than by a 'to'.

Nothing can be defined independently of the transcendental field. So all things must be thought of as in the field rather than as something it relates to. In Kant's case this false relation of 'to-ness' leads to a mistaken fixing of the transcendental in terms of the empirical. The transcendental is related to an empirical that in some way stands independent of it. In other words, the virtual becomes something we can identify and verify through its relation to the empirical.

The problem of this reference of the transcendental to something transcendent is that it illegitimately restricts the transcendental and thereby restricts the ways in which it can be actualised. The legislating function of the transcendental is particularly nefarious, if it is falsely defined according to some of the forms it is supposed to legislate and not others. Deleuze's reading of Kant is constantly critical of this conservative aspect of his thought, that is, that it reduces difference and imposes unchanging models against radical innovation and creativity because the transcendent cannot be broken with (despite its contingent empirical beginnings that are hidden in the application to the transcendental).

Second, this outer relation - where the transcendental is not thought of as 'in itself' but in relation to something else - is to a transcendent realm. Such a realm identifies its components, for example, in terms of invariant essences or conceptual properties. This means that a relation of subjection to identity is set up, where the processes of evolution and differentiation of the transcendental are limited through an external relation to the transcendent. Deleuze has a view of reality where all things are connected through differential variations. Transcendence curtails this variation in favour of identity.

When combined, these two points imply that the transcendental as condition is deduced and subordinated to a transcendence that is itself a fixing of the empirical. Conditions are sought for transcendent restrictions of the empirical: pure a priori conditions as well-determined identities. This then leads to a re-enforcement of that restriction as the conditions are then applied to any possible empirical case, in terms of how it must appear. Whilst the possibility of empirical cases requiring a revision or transformation of the conditions is eliminated by right.

It is possible, in the light of these remarks, to return to the critical questions addressed to Deleuze in the previous section. His departure from Kant on the transcendental is driven by a concern to use transcendental arguments and to define conditions in a philosophy of immanence. Kant's definition of the transcendental in terms of the a priori and in terms of a one-way legislation, rather than a reciprocal determination, dedicates transcendental arguments to transcendence.

This is because, in taking the pure form as his point of departure, and in taking the a priori as his point of arrival, Kant prejudges the transcendental and the empirical as transcendence. The pure form and the invariant a priori are illegitimately and subreptitiously drawn from prior identities, from Kantian ideas of the object or of the subject.

So, when Deleuze claims that Kant's transcendental reduplicates the empirical, he means that it is mirrored on a false, transcendent, view of the empirical. This explains why Deleuze can make the, at first sight absurd, claim of reduplication of the empirical, when Kant is at such pains to insist on a reduplication of a pure form. For Deleuze that form is still empirical, in the sense of the construction of a false transcendent form abstracted from a false form of subject and object.

The point of a Kantian transcendental deduction is to take an a priori form or law and a pure form or synthesis. It is then to draw a necessary line between the two, firstly, by showing that the form presupposes the a priori. Secondly, by concluding that the a priori is legislative for the pure form and for all empirical cases corresponding to it. But, from Deleuze's point of view, the points of departure involve a falsely manufactured transcendence with no legitimate empirical extension.

Experience and experimentation

In 'Immanence: a life...', Deleuze develops a distinction drawn between an immanent transcendental and transcendence, by qualifying his view of the transcendental according to the following points. This does not mean that the essay provides a full justification for the departure from Kant. Rather, it provides us with a partial explanation. Some of the points are very dense, since the essay is a beautiful attempt to condense ideas across Deleuze's career in a very short and elliptical manner.

1) The transcendental must be distinguished from experience;
2) The transcendental cannot be referred to an object of experience and it does not belong to the subject of an experience;
3) The transcendental is a 'pure flow of a-subjective pre-individual consciousness' or the 'qualitative duration' of consciousness;
4) There is a transcendental empiricism in opposition to an empiricism that presupposes a world of subjects and objects;
5) The power of the transcendental does not lie in an individual sensation, but in the passing from one sensation to another as an increase or decrease in power;
6) The relation of the transcendental field to consciousness is only by right, that is, in order to be determined, the field can be expressed in terms of consciousness but it need not be;
7) The transcendent is not the transcendental;
8) The transcendental is an absolute immanence - in itself and never in another or to another.

21

For Deleuze, if experience is thought of in terms of the experience of something by something, then the transcendental cannot be determined in terms of experience. More importantly, in wider definitions of experience, the transcendental is the condition for that which goes beyond the relation of an experiencing subject to an experienced object. His transcendental deductions are developed to find the conditions for what goes beyond the subject and object in a wider definition of life and experience (hence the title of his article). He therefore begins with events that resist the identifications associated with well-determined subjects and objects: pre-subjective sensations and the intensities associated with them.

There could be cause for confusion in this use of sensation. This is because Deleuze uses many different terms for sensibility as it occurs in actual events resistant to identification. In 'Immanence: a life…', he draws our attention to this resistance by defining sensation as the passage from one well-defined sensation to another. In *Difference and Repetition*, he sticks to the term sensation, but takes great care to avoid any connection to identity by associating sensation with the expression of virtual intensities. In *What is Philosophy?*, Guattari and Deleuze use terms such as percept and affect instead of sensation and perception. The constant in all these definitions is the disruptive power of sensation and its connection to the virtual. Sensation, or the passage from one sensation to another, cannot be identified, therefore, it presupposes transcendental conditions associated with becoming rather than being or essence.

In the late essay, he defines these conditions rather hermetically as a 'pure flow of a-subjective pre-individual consciousness'. To understand what he means by this, it is helpful to return to his earlier definition of the transcendental as 'Ideas' and 'intensities' from *Difference and Repetition*. These are virtual relations that can be expressed in terms of thought, but only where Ideas are not simply things that thinkers possess or contain, rather, they are something that individuals express, through what they say, do and write. Individuals access virtual Ideas that all of them connect to but express in individual ways. These Ideas are non-representational and they are not propositions (pure flows). They are not 'in' the mind of the thinker or the content of a thought (a-subjective and pre-individual).

The transcendental condition for sensations that cannot be identified along with subjects and objects are virtual Ideas that do not belong in any individual consciousness or to any individual subject and that cannot be associated with any identifiable object. Such Ideas are pure differences, as in free from any association with an empirical object. They are also mere qualitative flow, as in free from the boundaries and quantities associated with any given subject: 'the qualitative duration of consciousness'. For them to be otherwise would return the original unidentifiable sensations back to identity in the subject or in the object.

For Deleuze, experience and empiricism must be redefined in terms of the transcendental, because sensations presuppose virtual conditions (Ideas and intensities) that go beyond traditional Ideas of actual experience. Experimentation becomes the way in which the acts of individuals create with the expression of virtual Ideas and through virtual intensities. Empiricism is then not the identification of things as facts, it is the reconnection of illusory and temporary identifications with their transcendental conditions through sensations and experimentation with expression.

Life and experience are essentially experimental and, through sensations, associated with a creativity destructive of identity; each individual determines the transcendental in a singular way, whilst connecting to the different ways other individuals express that same transcendental field. This necessary role for individuality and experimentation, and the implied variability and multiplicity of the transcendental, runs counter to Kant's commitment to the a priori approached in terms of purity - a commitment to universality and to objectivity.

This explains Deleuze's many works on art, literature and cinema. They can be seen as essential aspects of the transcendental philosophy because they dramatise the sensations that Deleuze takes for his novel definition of experience. The art-works trigger limit-sensations that disturb well-ordered perceptions and make us aware of the mistaken identities and orderings that we use to keep the world stable and useable. In rendering the familiar unfamiliar and in taking our senses out of standard boundaries, the arts show that there is more to experience than what corresponds to well-determined concepts. They show that these concepts are insufficient in a radical way that necessitates reference to a virtual realm and to intensities that cannot be treated in terms of actual identifications - except at the cost of a false reduction and a pale illusion.

Deleuze's philosophy can be seen as an attempt to bring to life such illusions and to take us to a more complete view of reality. For him, the virtual and the actual enter into a relation of reciprocal determination that means that the transcendental no longer legislates for the actual. Instead, it provides grounds for views of reality in terms of completeness and incompleteness. A judgement or action will no longer be illegitimate, but incomplete with respect to the way it takes account of its virtual conditions. Deleuze never denies that we make identifications, either conceptually or in terms of perceptions. It is rather that, though necessary, these identifications are incomplete and damaging if left so.

In response to this new version of the critique of transcendental illusions, the Kantian criticism of this experimentation and of the transcendental defined in terms of singularity is that they lead to a contingent view of the transcendental a priori, to the point where it no longer seems to make sense to speak of the a priori at all. The transcendental is determined by experimentation and alters with it. Furthermore, if the transcendental is tied to singularity and singular experiments, is Deleuze then not committed to a kind of transcendental atomism, where each sensation is locked into its own transcendental with no communication to others?

Political and ethical consequences

In 'Immanence a life', Deleuze stages the ethical consequences of the transcendental-transcendence opposition through a series of examples that stress the value of virtual connections over actual differences. As persons, we are classified and recognised through our identifiable differences. We become objects for the judgements of others, not only through the initial judgement ascribing us to our particular differences, but also through subsequent judgements that place those differences in series of values. These values are themselves set in hierarchies and oppositions - good-evil, useful-useless, productive-redundant.

To illustrate this, Deleuze follows the description of the suffering of a rogue in Dickens' *Our Mutual Friend*. So long as the injured man is still alive enough to be recognised through his personality and the acts attached to it, the crook is still feared and despised by those around him. But as he fades away, and as his particularity disappears, suspicious onlookers start to work to save him. He becomes surrounded by respect and love for the last remains of life. Deep in his coma he senses this care. Yet, once the man starts to come round again, and once he starts to regain his distinctive and well-categorised features, 'his carers grow cold and all his coarseness and malevolence return.' (5, 171)

Deleuze's point is not that all men are equal and that no-one is truly a rogue. He often states that his view of difference is not that of the 'beautiful soul', where everything is apt to be saved through an indifferent aesthetic taste. As an actual particular character, the rogue remains a rogue. Rather, an impersonal transcendental life is expressed through every particular set of differences:

Between his life and death there is a moment which is now only that of a life playing with death. The life of the individual has given way to a life that is impersonal but singular nevertheless, and which releases a pure event freed from the accidents of inner and outer life; freed, in other words, from the subjectivity and objectivity of what happens: Homo tantum with which everyone sympathises and which attains a soil of beatitude. (5, 171)

To understand the ethical and political importance of this singular impersonal life, resistant to expression through identifications and judgements, and demanding a different set of ethical attitudes, it is important to return again to Deleuze's work on Kant in *Difference and Repetition*.

Deleuze is not worried about specific judgements made by Kant. Indeed, he is aware of Kant's revolutionary moves towards the transcendental subject and its capacity to undermine moves from particular empirical observations to false, dogmatic, definitions of human essences. Rather, Kant's critical philosophy is seen as remaining ethically and politically conservative despite its powerful discoveries with respect to the transcendental and to passivity with respect to transcendental conditions.

Deleuze's formal objection is that Kant still depends on representation - and hence on identity - through the importance of a meta-faculty of recognition. This conservatism is two-fold. It operates in the deduction of the a priori conditions for any given faculty. It also operates in the definition of the limits of all the faculties.

By insisting that pure a priori transcendental conditions must be deduced from pure general forms of phenomena, Kant subsumes the deductions to a faculty that allows us to recognise those pure general forms. We must be able to represent the form, that is, to identify it and to abstract it from empirical variation. It is then linked to an equally invariant and well-identified condition.

This is conservative because, according to Deleuze's view, variance is illegitimately removed from experience - in the a-subjective sense given above. It is also conservative because the faculty cannot adapt to different singularities. Instead, it subjects them to the legislation of universal a priori laws and categories.

Furthermore, the condition and form are recognised as different and particular to each faculty, thereby defining them as necessarily independent of each other in their transcendental invariance. Understanding cannot be reason. Reason cannot be aesthetic judgement. Again, this has conservative consequences for Deleuze, since faculties cannot change and thought becomes compartmentalised. Whereas, for him, thinking is a creative process where faculties evolve by transgressing their boundaries and interacting with others.

The contrast between the two transcendental philosophies is at its most stark here. It makes no sense, from Kant's position, for faculties to have a genealogy and to evolve. It makes no sense to speak of the transcendental in terms of singularity. His epistemological and ethical achievements would be fatally compromised were this the case.

This is because the categories of the understanding would be open to change and different for different individuals, thereby compromising his resistance to Hume's scepticism - not in the sense of the possibility of grounding knowledge against the problem of induction, but in the sense of undermining knowledge as legislated in the same way for all subjects. Understanding might remain, but not in the shared sense of objective knowledge.

The same applies to ethics, where the power of the categorical imperative to allow for subjects with different desires to bring them under one compatible system of maxims would be compromised. There would not be a single categorical imperative for all free rational subjects. Neither would there be a common reason to test whether maxims could be universalised.

We are therefore left with quite a stark opposition. Here is one of Deleuze's most critical statements against Kant's conservatism:

> We see to what degree the Kantian critique is ultimately respectful : knowledge, morality, are supposed to correspond to natural interests of reason, and are never themselves called into question. We only question the use of the faculties, that are declared legitimate according to one or other of these interests. (DR 137, 179)

It is answered by this more classically critical comment from Kant:

> In the absence of this critique reason is, as it were, in the state of nature, and can establish and secure its assertions and claims only through war. The critique, on the other hand, arriving at all its decisions in the light of the fundamental principles of its own institution, the authority of which no one can question, secures us a peace of a legal order, in which our disputes have to be conducted solely by the recognised methods of legal action. (CPR 601)

It is possible and worthwhile to discuss the merits on either side of this opposition in pragmatic terms. We could ask questions such as 'Which position allows for the most workable ethics?' and 'Which one fits best with current ways of understanding knowledge in the social sciences?' However, in the more abstract context of the difference between transcendental philosophies, it is helpful to make the following points:

1) Deleuze's position does not imply that he should oppose all laws and maxims, rather, his philosophy commits him to an openness and experimentation with respect to them. Flexibility, critical challenges right to the core of any moral and political system, and radical openness to different views would be the guidelines for a Deleuzian take on enlarging the enlightenment project.

2) When Deleuze accuses Kant of conservatism, he is making a philosophical rather than practical or empirical point. There are relations between them, but these will be very hard to trace through to actual cases. Instead, the accusation is more at the level of principles and models for thought, rather than actual empirical interventions. Much work remains to be done by both philosophies in terms of bringing critique and creative openness into practical politics and social practices, such that neither could be accurately called conservative in specific situations. In fact, when differences in epochs are taken into account, neither philosopher's practical political positions could reasonably be called conservative when compared with the respective philosophical mainstreams.

3) The opposition between Kant and Deleuze could therefore be thought of as a struggle for the legacy of enlightenment. Should critique be taken further and extended to the role of recognition and of the faculties? Or does this extension lose enlightenment values, perhaps even collapsing into nonsense, because transcendental philosophy can be taken too far, in particular in the denial of the permanence of important transcendental distinctions between legitimate realms and of the categories that hold within them. In short, how experimental and contingent on individual experience can the enlightenment project become before it loses any coherence? To answer these questions it is important to look at the theoretical oppositions in greater detail, in particular, with a view to truth and validity.

Transcendental Ideas, possibility and truth

Deleuze and Kant share a commitment to the transcendental and to transcendental deductions. Deleuze's work on the virtual and his definition of transcendental Ideas in *Difference and Repetition* is explicitly Kantian. To a lesser extent this is true of his work on passivity, in terms of time and in relation to the subject (also in *Difference and Repetition* but also elsewhere, for example, in the two volumes on cinema).

However, as we have seen, the two thinkers diverge on the form of the transcendental, due to different views of the given. This leads to different conclusions on the relation of the transcendental to the phenomenal, in Kant, and on the asymmetrical reciprocal determination of virtual and actual, for Deleuze. For the former, the identity of the phenomenon is mirrored by the identity and fixity of the transcendental conditions. For the latter, the non-identifiable variation of sensation is mirrored by a pure variation in the transcendental.

For Kant, the relation of condition to phenomenon is legislating, that is, it sets the limits of legitimate propositions for a given faculty with respect to phenomena. For Deleuze the virtual and the actual change with one another. The genesis of new sensations and hence new structures in the actual depend on changes in the virtual. The relations between virtual Ideas depend on the emergence of new sensations in the actual. This explains Deleuze's insistence on the term 'reciprocal determination'.

An investigation of the roots of the two positions in terms of their presuppositions regarding identity in the phenomenon and difference in sensation would be one way of trying to settle the opposition between them. However, given that Deleuze's position depends on a dramatisation of sensation that appeals to an aesthetic sense, and given that it could be argued that Kant's commitment to identity and to the possibility of a pure general form rests on a similar but more deeply hidden appeal to the form in imagination, it is far from obvious how any debate could go beyond competing ways of staging experiences of difference or of identity.

It is perhaps more interesting to look beyond these presuppositions to their consequences, in particular, with respect to what they commit us to with respect to views of reality. This is especially important, since transcendental philosophies already commit us to surprising, if not downright counter-intuitive views of reality through the reality of the non-empirical transcendental condition. This explains why the oppositions between Deleuze and Lewis, discussed in other chapters, are so important. Lewis puts forward a metaphysics that resists transcendental turns and pays much greater heed to intuition or common sense, thereby setting up a counter-position to Kant and to Deleuze.

In terms of this counter to common sense, Deleuze seems to be far more demanding than Kant, since Deleuze allows for a quasi-causal relation with the transcendental - albeit in an unknowable manner (we know that there is a relation of reciprocal determination but we cannot know actual chains of determination). Both thinkers discuss one such consequence in their work on possibility. Deleuze does so with the explicit intention of separating his work on Ideas from Kant's. This difference in treatments of possibility is important, since it leads to different reactions to Lewis's position and its basis in possible worlds and modal logic.

Kant's work on possibility is concerned to cleave between legitimate and illegitimate teleological propositions in terms of the purposiveness or design of nature and in terms of shared judgements of taste. These propositions are themselves responses to the antinomies that arise from the separation of faculties (of reason, judgement and the understanding). For reason, it is legitimate to assume that nature is purposive and even that there is a designer - they are legitimate possibilities. For the understanding, we can never know that there is such a purpose or creator - they are not possible. In terms of judgements of taste, an aesthetic judgement shared by all is a possibility, but any given judgement of taste cannot command assent by all (*Critique of Judgement*, 56).

In *Difference and Repetition*, having acknowledged his closeness to Kant, Deleuze goes on to explain the great difference between them. Kant is right to deduce the necessity of Ideas. He is also right to show how Ideas can go beyond the understanding and, hence, on to founding a truly problematic realm of Ideas, that is, one that does not allow for straightforward empirical or categorical counters. But Kant still fixes Ideas and problems, thereby retaining truth and falsehood - both thought in terms of identifiable forms.

The following passage is poignant, since Deleuze situates Kant close to all he holds highest in *Difference and Repetition* - to dialectics and to thought as a form of problematisation. But then Kant is accused of the dogmatism he fought so hard to avoid:

[Kant's] profound theory of Ideas as problematising and problematic allowed him to rediscover the real source of the dialectic, and even to introduce problems into the geometric exposition of Practical Reason. However, because the Kantian critique remains dominated by common sense or the dogmatic image, Kant still defines the truth of a problem in terms of the possibility of its finding a solution: this time it is a question of a transcendental form of possibility, in accordance with a legitimate use of the faculties as this is determined in each case by this or that organisation of common sense (to which the problem corresponds). (DR 161, 209)

Most of Deleuze's criticisms and differences are here. Kant depends on a 'common sense' committed to identity above difference, a 'dogmatic image' of thought based on identity in representation. Thought is not allowed to be an open process in relation to irresolvable problems. Instead, it is subjected to tribunals that determine what is legitimate for propositions ascribed to this or that faculty.

But Deleuze's criticism is deeper than these rather stark remarks and their equally stark opposites (All experience is of difference not sameness. Creative thought is about overcoming boundaries set in terms of identity. Faculties can transcend their set limits.) His point is that, where questions of truth and falsity are concerned, Kant sets Ideas up as secondary to other faculties. An Idea is never real, only possible, until it corresponds to a concept of the understanding, that is, until it is subjected to a rule of identity. This explains the distinction drawn between the possibility of universal assent in terms of judgements of taste and actual disagreements. The Idea of universal assent is merely possible and cannot be verified conceptually, but only in practice and partially ('The universal voice is therefore only an idea...' CJ, 56).

It is this 'only' an idea that worries Deleuze, since he wants to claim that Ideas are real and operate on the actual all the time but to different degrees. His opposition to possibility in terms of Ideas and transcendental philosophy is therefore that it misses the ongoing reciprocal determination of the virtual and the actual or of the transcendental and what we take to be actually given. Ideas, in Deleuze's sense, are at work even when we are not conscious of them. It is not a matter of whether we use them correctly or not (as if it were possible not to use them). It is matter of how our actions determine all Ideas in different ways and whether this constitutes a life-affirming expression of them or not. That is why Deleuze's ideas cannot be separable identifiable entities; they must be interconnected and inseparable relations that become determined in different ways in accordance with the different degrees of intensity of the relations. We bring Ideas to the fore and relegate others to a background where they are still operative but to a lesser degree. We do not select an Idea and make it actual, leaving others as mere possibilities.

For Deleuze, all Ideas are real. They should only be distinguished in terms of how powerfully they come into play through any given sensation and within an individual. So Kant's error is to think that Ideas can be judged in terms of whether a legitimate concept of the understanding corresponds to them or whether they are subjectively necessary. When, in fact, the right questions with respect to Ideas are about selection and degrees of emphasis in response to individual events and sensations. Not 'Is this Idea legitimate and according to which faculty?' but 'How is this problem operating in the constitution of this singular event and how should I select it in the creation of new partial solutions to it?'

For Kant, such talk of singularity is absurd, since there are ways of deciding about subjective necessity and objective truth. There is neither mere singularity and individuality, nor the freedom to select independent of truth and falsehood: 'Reason is a power of principles, and its ultimate demand aims at the unconditioned. Understanding, on the other hand, always serves reason only under a certain condition, one that must be given. But without concepts of the understanding, to which objective reality must be given, reason cannot make objective judgements at all.' *Critique of Judgement*, 284

This explains why Deleuze develops a strong critique of concepts and properties in *Difference and Repetition*. If Kant is right and concepts are a necessary shackle on the unconditioned aim of reason, then Deleuze cannot maintain his claim about the necessary connection and reciprocal determination of Ideas and actual things. Deleuze's answer is that objective judgements and concepts of the understanding are always incomplete, if considered in abstraction from Ideas, that is, in abstraction from a transcendental realm that does not allow for the separation of faculties and realms. Where Kant argues that objective reality must be given to concepts of the understanding, thereby providing objective boundaries for reason, Deleuze counters that it makes no sense to speak of objective reality, since reality does not allow for such sub-divisions. The concept is part of the Idea and the Idea is part of the concept in such a way as to make any claim based on their independence impossible. There is no neutral, intensity-free, Idea-independent concept.

Deleuze and Kant's philosophies can never be reconciled on these points. This is because, from similar roots in transcendental deductions, but from different commitments to pure formal identity and to pure virtual differences, they arrive at fundamentally different views. This extends to the role of principles in philosophy. Kant arrives at regulative and constitutive principles, whereas Deleuze works with temporary pragmatic ones. For one, principles are rigid limits for thought. For the other, they can only be a tentative and transitory part of an experimental creative process.

Notes

1) My thanks go to Rachel Jones for her clarifications on this point and also on Kant's relation to Hume (see her'"You Kantian!': Feminist Interpretations of Kant', *Women's Philosophy Review*, Issue 28, 2001-2, pp. 22-84).

3

Deleuze and Levinas:
towards an ethics of expression

Expressionism as ground for an ethical relation

In the *Tractatus*, Wittgenstein famously draws a distinction between saying and showing: 'What can be shown cannot be said.'[1] Deleuze's *Difference and Repetition* adds a third term and an important valuation to the distinction. The most powerful things, things without which life is incomplete, can only be expressed. They are beyond the resources of both saying and showing. An individual is always more than what it knows and what it does. Indeed, what the individual knows and what it does only reach their full sense in expression: 'Expression is installed at the heart of the individual, in its body and in its soul, in its passions and in its actions, in its causes and in its effects.'[2]

Expression is to be the realm of aesthetics. This should not surprise us. Deleuze sets an aesthetic dramatisation at the heart of his philosophy. His accounts of art insist on the expressive power of works over and above what they can represent.[3] Indeed, through the distinction drawn between representation and expression, his claim goes beyond Wittgenstein's saying and his showing. Expressive art only exceeds representation when the expressed thing is not present - even as something that can only be shown. For when it can be shown it returns too readily to the dominion of the concept and the realm of the said.

More surprising, though, is Deleuze's claim that ethical relations are also a matter of expression rather than of a pragmatic showing, of a conceptual understanding or of an experience of transcendence. Towards the end of the last main chapter of *Difference and Repetition*, Deleuze strives to distinguish the expressive ethical relation from inter-subjective relations in Sartre's existentialism. When ethics is thought of as a relation between subjects, it becomes mired in an oscillation around asymmetrical subject-object relations.[4] As a subject, I am always forced to objectify the other subject - the other becomes an object. But, in the presence of the other subject, of her gaze, for example, I become aware of her active subjectivity and of my position as an object with respect to it - I become an object.

So we have to internalise a difficult tension where, in Sartre's words, '...no synthesis of these two forms is possible'.[5] We are both subject and object, in a way that can neither be transcended through an appeal to a common rationality or to a common language, nor through an appeal to relations that come before the subject and the object and that belie their apparent differences. Representational communication presupposes active communicators and passive referents, thereby replicating the subject-object distinction. A pre-subjective flesh or phenomenological relation fails at its frontiers: how does it relate to the history of subjects and objects? How does it relate to their future? The concept of expression takes us beyond the subject-object distinction, but with no recourse to a denial of their effective reality.

Deleuze describes a relation between individuals that are neither merely subjects nor merely objects, nor both. Instead, individuals are expressive perspectives on the whole of reality - they are the whole of reality, including subjects and objects, under different perspectives. So the ethical relation between individuals lies in the way each expression interferes with another and is in turn interfered with. In his favoured term, individuals and their perspectives are folded into one another.[6] Ethically, individuals do not communicate with one another; in the sense where that communication would be viewed as the transference of an identifiable package (*Did you get it?*) But neither do they exist under a transcendent law barring the other from any communication or relation (*This is an absolute Other, to be respected in its otherness*). Rather, a reciprocal movement occurs in the related individuals. So there is a relation. But the relation as movement cannot be traced in causal terms. There are no laws governing the relation. Neither does it have an identifiable content. There is no sense of foundational shared truths, sensations or facts; such things are only ever incomplete parts of reality and therefore mistaken grounds for thinking about ethical relations. This is not an ethics as science, nor an ethics as transcendent religious or quasi-religious relation.[7]

Deleuze describes the ethical situation of individuals thus: 'In every psychic system there is a swarm of possibilities around reality, but our possibles are always Others. The Other cannot be separated from the expressivity which constitutes it.'[8] A first stab at interpreting this claim is that Deleuze views reality as mobile, as a changing and open-ended relation between a psychic system (sensations, perceptions, structural relations between concepts, physical and chemical functions) and a wider reality: 'It is the brain that says I, but I is another... sensation is no less brain than the concept'.[9] This mobility is articulated through others. To understand this claim further, we must turn to the detail of Deleuze's doctrine of individuals.

As individuals 'we' have certainties in the form of identifiable truths and knowledge (including what we take to be true about ourselves) but these are only significant for us through our singular relations to the known and to the true. These relations are sensations. Of all the facts that come to make up your world why are some closer to you than others, why do some matter and others recede, since all are equally true as objects of knowledge? It is because you are more than what you know. You are what you feel. But you are not simply what you perceive, for that is related to the known.[10] You are what you sense over and above what you perceive (*This is what defines me, and no fact can explain its importance*).[11]

Sensation is not the identification of a body of knowledge but the transformation of that body through feelings that make it individual and resistant to the parity of the true. Sensation is therefore the site for two movements. First, when we are taken as identifiable objects, it moves us, ceaselessly keeping us away from a simple reduction to the known (*This is who you are, just as it appear on the census - this is what you will do, just as it is predicted in the laws that govern your kind*). Second, sensation is movement in itself, an inner resistance to identification. If it were not, then it would fall back into a system of representation and knowledge (*It is our faculties of hearing and sight, but my ear, eye, love, hate*). A perception is identifiable, but it is fatally general.[12] A sensation undoes identification, but its singularity remains beyond compare - on its own, psychology is doomed to tell us much about what matters little.

But if knowledge can tell us nothing of sensations, how can we live with them? How can we do justice to them? How can they become part of the unfolding of our lives and of our plans to live a life well? For Deleuze, other individuals teach us how to live. The way their sensations express an invisible side to the world allows us to learn how to live with our own sensations and with the hidden side that sets us in motion. We learn about our sensations, what they have in store for us, and what we can do with them, through the special sensations triggered by another individual.

The other individual is itself tested by a singular perspective on an obscure side of a world that each must express in a singular way.[13] In *Difference and Repetition*, Deleuze gives one example of this ethical relation:

Consider a terrified face (under conditions such that I do not see and do not experience the causes of this terror). This face expresses a possible world: the terrifying world. By "expression" we mean, as always, that relation which involves a torsion between an expressor and an expressed such that the expressed does not exist apart from the expressor, even though the expressor relates to it as though to something completely different. By "possible", therefore, we do not mean any resemblance but that state of the implicated or enveloped in its very heterogeneity with what envelops it: the terrified face does not resemble what terrifies it, it envelops a state of the terrifying world.[14]

Prior to considering the ethical implications of this passage, it is important to undo false impressions that may follow from it. First, the face here is but an example of an expressor, it should not be privileged through the assumption that Deleuze's individuals are human individuals. On the contrary, there is an individual wherever there is sensation and expression; the human is but a case and maybe a distortion of this definition of the individual.

Second, in line with the critique of the possible developed in the Lewis and Kant chapters here, Deleuze does not mean that reality is made up of series of real possible worlds. Instead, his use of possible here is a description of the experience of seeing the terrified face. We think and sense a possible world that in reality was always a real virtual one - just one that we did not see. The possible world in this sense is not one that could be selected and judged in totality with respect to other possible worlds. The possible world is *part* of my world, not a possibility *for* it; from Deleuze's point of view, it only makes sense to call it possible in describing the experience of discovering something latent that we did not sense before, rather than implying a claim that the possible is a key ontological property of worlds.

Deleuze and Levinas on the face and the Other

Deleuze's example of an ethical relation is striking in its similarities but also in its contrasts to Emmanuel Levinas's work on the Other and the face in *Totality and Infinity* and, to a lesser extent, in *Otherwise than Being or Beyond Essence*.[15] Both thinkers view the face as a barrier to comprehension, but the reasons it stands as an obstacle are very different.[16] For Levinas, the face cannot be grasped because something of the face, and of the face alone, transcends reason and understanding:

The face is present in its refusal to be contained. In this sense, it cannot be comprehended, that is, encompassed. It is neither seen nor touched - for in visual or tactile sensation the identity of the I envelopes the alterity of the object, which becomes precisely a content.[17]

For Deleuze, on the other hand, the face does not transcend alone. It only does so through a particular external 'condition', that is, the absence of the world that sets it in motion. This does not mean that this condition can be separated from the face, on the contrary, he insists on the dependence of expressed and expressor - their 'torsion' or the way they set off twists in each other. However, this interdependence means that neither the expressed, nor the expressor can be charged solely with the ethical task of relating individuals to what they differently, but commonly, express through their sensations.

It could be claimed, though, that a condition and torsion is also a factor in Levinas's argument, to the extent that speech reveals the transcendent in the presence of the Other:

If the transcendent cuts across sensibility, if it is openness pre-eminently, if its vision is the vision of the very openness of being, it cuts across the vision of forms and can be stated neither in terms of contemplation nor in terms of practice. It is the face; its revelation is speech.[18]

But speech is wedded to the face in its resistance to transcendence: no face, no transcendence. For Deleuze, on the other hand, this privileging of a particular *there* (the face or, perhaps, the caress)[19] and, therefore, of a particular form of expression (speech) is a false restriction of expression. What matters, is not a special existence - the face as that which transcends our ability to grasp it as phenomenon or object - but a special relation.

This relation is four-fold and takes the form world-sensation-dramatisation-world or in the language of Deleuze's example: world-sensation-terror-world. There is no possible reduction of any of the points of the relation to any other, that is, each is of the form expressor and expressed, where the two cannot be separated but, equally, where they must remain distinct for expression to take place. By dramatisation Deleuze means a new way of playing a given relation of expression and expressed, that is, like the director putting a new version of a play, the expressor must take something that already determines this version, but that must also be given a new and re-invigorating slant. Dramatisation is therefore a more detailed version of expression, taking account of the expression of virtual relations of 'Ideas' and 'intensities' in actual differences: 'This intensive field of individuation determines the relations that it expresses to be incarnated in spatio-temporal dynamisms (dramatisation), in species which correspond to these relations (specific differenciation), and in organic parts which correspond to the distinctive points in these relations (organic differenciation).'[20]

The dramatisation determines the world and the world determines the dramatisation in a relation of reciprocal determination, as one changes so does the other in an interminable and irreducible circle that includes all individuals. In *Difference and Repetition*, reciprocal determination is the technical term for torsion, or the way two things are related through a shared twist, each expressing the force exercised at the other end[21] (*What is my world without her, what is my world without him?*) But what is ethical about this relation, in the sense of what is to be valued about the relation? Why is it important for us to understand this relation as ethical, rather than work with a (maybe) less truthful one, but one that is more easy to operate, or to align with morality?

The force of these critical questions can be understood in their application to Deleuze's explanation of how individuals should respond to problems (including ones raised in ethical situations). Problems should be counter-actualised, that is, replayed and dramatised in different ways. This means that there are no lasting solutions, as if problems were questions allowing for right answers, but it also seems to imply that we should treat others, and ethical problems that involve them, as we would treat a theatrical part and fellow actors. This would introduce the possibility of an unwelcome instrumentality and lack of authenticity to ethical relations, either in terms of treating others as secondary to my performance, or in terms of judging both my performance and those of others as secondary to an external audience (which could either be others or another version of my self).

Starting with the face, Levinas leads us to an ethics of unconditional obligation, but Deleuze seems to have given us either a value-free structure or an instrumental one. Levinas sets out a privileged *there* and hence allows us to think through some of the most important and enduring problems of morality (on murder, respect, war and discrimination, among others):

> The impossibility of killing does not have a simple negative and formal signification; the relation with infinity, the idea of infinity in us conditions it positively. Infinity presents itself as a face in the ethical resistance that paralyses my powers and from the depths of defenceless eyes rises firm and absolute in its nudity and destitution.[22]

To mediate the infinity of the face by describing it as a mediator between an individual and an unseen world, as Deleuze does, seems to inhibit its power to paralyse. Each face becomes determined through what it expresses and its resistance is broken down through our turn away from it and towards the expressed. When the face becomes the way to our possibilities, it appears to take on an hypothetical role - an individual becomes a means for another (*I love you for your story alone*).

Deleuze speaks of the possibilities conveyed through the other's terror, but he appears to make no judgement as to the value of that possibility - or, more properly, that latent set of virtual relations. Neither does he ascribe intrinsic values to the terms that allow that latency to be expressed (*What if I am the cause of that terror? What if I choose to cause that terror, to reveal my possibilities?*)[23] Is terror to be privileged, or can the triggering sensation be love, or hate? Yet he does have something like an ethical principle in mind in his example. It recurs through *Difference and Repetition* and is stated again soon after the example on terror. We should not 'explicate oneself too much with the other' and not 'explicate the other too much.'[24] We should resist the temptation to explain the terror through an identification of the world that sets it off, or through an identification of my terror with the terror experienced by the other individual.

This helps us to understand why Deleuze defines possibility against resemblance and with heterogeneity. As possible, the expressed world is not like the world we know, or like a world we could know. As terror, the sensation undergone by the other is nothing like my terror. Rather, the expression shows us that there are worlds that operate on us that we cannot know, only express. This expression requires expressors: we have to explicate, but not too much. This is nothing like the revealed certainty of the infinite as ethical resistance in Levinas in its provision for obligation. Though the two positions share a situation of the Other as beyond the grasp of reason and the understanding, Deleuze's position appears to break with the Levinasian resistance through relative explications of the Other. Is Deleuze's ethics, then, a turn away from obligation and back to the hypothetical treatment of the Other?

In *Totality and Infinity*, Levinas rejects this reduction of the Other to a means under the guise of Hegelian or Spinozist idealism: 'The Other and the I function as elements of an ideal calculus, receive from this calculus their real being, and approach one another under the dominance of ideal necessities which traverse from all sides.'[25] He rejects it because the dominance fails to take account of the infinite otherness expressed with the face and thereby allows the other to become a means. The calculation depends on comparisons and equivalences that destroy otherness by mediating it.

It is therefore very important to consider whether Deleuze's statements on calculus as central to his philosophy fall prey to Levinas's powerful criticisms. Here is Deleuze's key statement on his calculus from *Difference and Repetition*:

> If Ideas are the differentials of thought, there is a differential calculus corresponding to each Idea, an alphabet of what it means to think. Differential calculus is not the unimaginative calculus of the utilitarian, the crude arithmetic calculus which subordinates thought to other things or to other ends, but the algebra of pure thought, the superior irony of problems themselves - the only calculus 'beyond good and evil'. [26]

Must we understand this 'higher calculus,'[27] with its Spinozist roots, as leading to the dominance of the Other by necessity? In order to answer these questions it is essential to return to the detail of Deleuze's and Levinas's positions on expression and infinity, in particular because Deleuze's philosophy claims to escape comparison (in repetition, for example) and equivalence (in the pure difference of intensity, for example). Yet these claims seem to clash with the comments on higher calculus. Can Deleuze define expression without presupposing a form of mediation? Which thinker defines infinity best in terms of a resistance to comparison and equivalence?

Expression in speech and expression as drama

Does the distinction drawn between Levinas's *there* of the face and Deleuze's expressivity in terror exaggerate their differences? In *Totality and Infinity*, Levinas describes the face both as an expression and as the expression of the Other in speech. The face is infinite because in speech, face to face, the Other exceeds my grasp:

> The expression the face introduces into the world does not defy the feebleness of my powers, but my ability for power. The face, still a thing among things, breaks through the form that nevertheless delimits it. This means concretely: the face speaks to me and thereby invites me to a relation incommensurate with a power exercised, be it enjoyment or knowledge.[28]

This incommensurability also holds for Deleuze's structure. It is because the face is expressive and because it expresses a world beyond my grasp that the relation is one of incommensurability. This lack of measure is all-important for his definition of sensation as the expression of an intensity that must be beyond measure: 'Intensity is both the imperceptible and that which can only be sensed.'[29]

But, despite these similarities, profound differences persist between the two thinkers. They concern the key concepts, structure and method of the philosophies. First, in terms of concepts, the following point of divergence stands out. Irrespective of its role in the validity of Levinas's arguments and of its wider importance for his philosophy, a precise and restricting vocabulary - of religious origin - dominates his description of the face in relation to speech. The face stands at the limit between 'holiness and caricature' and speech is the 'epiphany' of the infinite in the face: 'The epiphany of the face is ethical. The struggle this face can threaten *presupposes* the transcendence of expression.'[30] This invocation of religious manifestation is important because it sets speech and the face in relation to an infinite that can only be revealed and never grasped. Expression, therefore, must be thought of in terms of a world that will always be beyond our capacity to map out and predict. In speech, the Other necessarily eludes us and thereby puts us in a state of obligation: 'This infinity, stronger than murder, already resist us in his face, is his face, is the primordial *expression*, is the first word: "You shall not commit murder."'[31]

So the appeal to epiphany in relation to the infinite sets Levinas's ethics in a very precise and restricted relation. The epiphany must take place in the face because it is the privileged site for that epiphany. The expression revealed in the face must be the infinite defined as the 'infinity of transcendence' or, in more concrete terms, as an 'unforeseeableness'.[32] So, though Levinas cautions us to avoid confusing epiphany with a mystical relation and with rite and liturgy,[33] and though it would be a mistake to think that the difference between Deleuze and Levinas lies in the trite fact that one uses religious terminology and one avoids it, through epiphany the concept of expression is associated with an extraordinary event in Levinas. This extraordinary event is in turn tied to the revelation of infinity where it is defined as an excess over what can be grasped - a transcendence.[34]

Levinas returns to the concept of epiphany in terms of the infinite in *Otherwise than Being or Beyond Essence*. Again, the infinite as transcendence is thought of through speech and through an opposition drawn between the saying (speech) and the said (discourse about being/propositions of knowledge). Speech is the epiphany of transcendence, not only because the possibility of speech by the Other must always turn my grasp of it into something perpetually provisional, but also because my speech becomes a provisional and transcended response to the Other's provocation: 'The transcendence of the revelation lies in the fact that the "epiphany" comes in the saying of him that received it.[35] This insistence on speech, the face and the infinite in the primacy of ethics is not the delimitation of a realm separate from all others, since ethics is the condition for the emergence of ontology. However, this primacy of ethics, defined according to epiphany, depends on a necessarily restricted set of phenomena, for example, in terms of those that convey the epiphany, due to their provisional nature, and those that belie epiphany in translating the infinite as said.

In contrast, the character and style of Deleuze's work is to multiply examples of expression and to insist on the range of disciplines that can lead us to individuals - the terrified face is only an example that becomes the face of fear in Deleuze's article on otherness and Michel Tournier in *The Logic of Sense*.[36] There is no privileged field of individuals or privileged expressive sensation, what matters is the structure of expressed and expressor, not how that structure is instantiated. Deleuze argues that space is suffused with individual differences that give it different senses: 'The form of the field must be necessarily and in itself filled with individual differences. This plenitude must be immediate, thoroughly precocious and not delayed in the egg, to such a degree that the principle of individuals would indeed have the formula given to it by Lucretius: no two eggs or grains of wheat are identical.'[37] Individuals occur with sensations that are signs of movements beyond the known and beyond what has already become identified. The reference to the egg is a reaction to the argument that sensual intensities defining individuals have a privileged location where genetic transformation is at its most open - the egg or embryo. There is no such privileged location, there are individuals wherever there is sensation, and there must be sensation wherever there are significant differences, that is, everywhere - even in grains of sand.

This discussion of the multiple sites for individuals and sensation occurs in chapter 5 of *Difference and Repetition*, where Deleuze defines the concept of intensity in the context of a resistance to the priority given to diversity or recognisable differences in the sciences, for example, to species in biology. His argument is that individuals are determined by their sensations and intensities. These cannot be thought of as identifiable as well-determined facts or pre-determined by the forms of given categories (as if the fact of belonging to a particular species limited the intensities that could run through and transform an individual). Part of his argument is that radical change and evolution take place outside the boundaries of species and these come later and are secondary to the creative evolutions that make and unmake them. Individuals are prior and cross the boundaries of categories that are supposed to determine their properties and of perceptions that are supposed to determine their capacity to interact with their environment.

John Llewelyn argues that individuality in Levinas cannot be referred to the multiple in the Leibnizian (and, therefore, Deleuzian)[38] sense because this would mediate the relation of individual to Other through a system. Levinas's individuals emerge in the facing towards the Other as a prior ethical relation: 'Ethical individuality prior to ontic individuality is due not to participation but to facing, in which each individual before individuality is a unique me facing and faced by a unique Other beyond conceptuality.'[39] But this view overlooks the possibility that individuals can be multiple through their perspective on the world and set in motion through relations with others, but without the possibility of system. Indeed, this is one of the main metaphysical advancements of Deleuze's thought. With a new and deeper interpretation of Spinoza and Leibniz, and against a restrictive Hegelian understanding,[40] he proposes a structure of reality that involves a multiplicity of relations that undoes any emerging system:

> What is missed [by the definition of problems in terms of a field of possible solutions] is the internal character of the problem as such, the imperative internal element which decides in the first place its truth or falsity and measures its intrinsic power: that is, the very object of the dialectic or combinatory, the 'differential'. Problems are tests and selections. What is essential is that there occurs at the heart of problems a genesis of truth, a production of the true in thought.[41]

There is difference at the heart of the Deleuzian structure, itself thought of in terms of problems that undo systematic thought and call for an open creative selection. He calls this creation a dramatisation (*How shall I play my life to bring it in counter-point with the world the other has expressed?*)

Movement, structure, infinity

Deleuze's appeal to creation and to selection leads to the structural difference between Levinas's and Deleuze's studies of the face and expression. The difference is not so much a matter of the number of terms in the relation, since it could be argued that both are triangular: with nodes corresponding to face, speech and face in Levinas and to expressed, expressor and sensation in Deleuze. Though I argued above that Deleuze's structure was four-fold, the two instances of the world as that which is expressed could be conflated, with the remark that they are different perspectives of the same thing. That they are not depends on the property of the relation in terms of transformations.

43

For Deleuze, each of the terms expressed, expressor, sensation is deter-mined by the other, that is, each is profoundly transformed by the other. For Levinas, the relation is blocked in an important direction: from the subject in the presence of the face, to the face and its possibility of speech as epiphany. Levinas describes false moves in that direction, as if the ethical obligation brought on by the face of the Other could be cancelled in killing, objectification or subjection, or as if the face could be treated like a phenomenon that carried information. But none of these impositions can touch the face as epiphany, where the face is always beyond any given identification as phenomenon or, indeed, manifestation; 'To manifest oneself as a face is to impose oneself above and beyond the manifested and purely phenomenal form, to present oneself in a mode irreducible to manifestation, the very straightforwardness of the face to face, without the intermediary of any image...'[42] Though the face is manifestation, to identify it as such and hence to fuse the manifestation with infinity is not possible.

Levinas's ethical relation is not a denial of the ways in which obligation can appear to be by-passed in the rationalisation of the Other. It is a denial of the possibility of reducing the Other to the same, to a rationalisation of it, despite appearances. This is because the ethical relation comes prior to rea-son and to an ontology that grasps the meaning of being: 'Preexisting the disclosure of being in general taken as the basis of knowledge and as mean-ing of being is the relation with the existent that expresses himself; pre-exist-ing the plane of ontology is the ethical plane.'[43] Thus one is not free of the obligation when one ignores it. Even in ignoring it we testify to it as the condition for our ignorance - to seek to kill the Other is testimony to the Other's transcendence over us and to the possibility of speech that murder tries to eliminate.[44] For Levinas, we can never 'have done' with ethics, defined as the responsibility and obligation in the face of the Other. This is because the infinite manifested in that relation always remains beyond our grasp: 'The subject is inspired by the infinite, which as illeity [the *there* of the face], does not appear, is not present, has always already passed, is neither theme, telos, nor interlocutor.'[45]

Deleuze reverses this Levinasian prioritisation of ethics over ontology. For him, a truly differential ontology must underpin even the possibility of ethics. This ontology responds to Levinas's objection to the role of identity, representation and totality in ontology understood in terms of the said; '[The said] is already a hypostasis of the eon,[46] and the source of a subreption that limits what is thought to essence and to reminiscence (that is, to synchronic time and representation)...'[47] It does so by claiming that a difference resistant to representation is the condition for identity and representation. It is worth noting that the priority of difference over ethics is also asserted by Jean-François Lyotard in his reading of Levinas in *The Differend*. The differend between different phrase regimens is prior to the infinite obligation that occurs with the face of the other. This is not to deny this obligation, but to set it among many different types of relation and phrase-regimen with no rule over them.[48]

A key to this priority of ontology over ethics lies in Deleuze's unflinching commitment to univocity in ontology (being is said in the same way for all things). In opposing an Aristotelian ontology, Deleuze claims, in *Difference and Repetition*, that difference - understood as the multiple in the individual - is the condition for species and ontological categories: 'We must show not only how individuating difference differs in kind from specific difference, but primarily and above all how individuation precedes matter and form, species and parts, and every other element of the constituted individual.'[49] 'To be' is not simply an empty term that must be supplemented by a series of different 'to be an X'. In other words, all things are in the same way and this way has a full sense as 'to be as differing or becoming'. It is therefore not an empty category that only acquires sense once it is divided further (in *Difference and Repetition*, this statement comes out of a development of ontological positions taken from Scotus, Spinoza and Nietzsche). The ontology at stake here is highly complex and rests on a series of difficult transcendental arguments.[50] In *Difference and Repetition*, Deleuze's claim for a univocal ontology brings together actual identities, sensations, virtual intensities and virtual ideas in a series of unbreakable reciprocal determinations. This means that no view of a thing is complete unless it brings together virtual and actual sides, sensations and ideas.

Furthermore, the realm of the virtual allows for no legitimate subdivisions of its elements. The whole of Ideas[51] is determined solely by relations of greater and lesser clarity and obscurity. The whole of intensities is determined by relations of folding or perplication. Individuals imply singular relations of clarity and obscurity and of perplication. So, for Deleuze, all things are individuals or incomplete parts of individuals defined as reciprocal relations between Ideas, intensities, sensations and actual identities. Any individual is an expression of all Ideas, though more or less clearly and obscurely. It is an expression of all intensities, though in different configurations of envelopment. Through the Ideas it expresses and the intensities that envelop it, an individual's actual side is connected to all other actual things (there is a fuller account and defence of this claim and of its transcendental grounds in my chapter on Kant and Deleuze).

The key point for the separation of individuals from representation and the said lies in the definition of Ideas as multiplicities of relations between elements that defy identification. Deleuze defines an Idea as an 'n-dimensional well-defined and continuous multiplicity,'[52] where the dimension is the number of variations and where the variations are continuous, that is, involve no discrete steps. The insistence on continuity is supplemented by a series of conditions concerning the impossibility of identifying the elements of the multiplicity and by proofs regarding the necessity of Ideas. Together, they ensure that a pure difference becomes the condition for any representation and a necessary component of the complete view of any individual. In return, though, sensation in relation representation and identity becomes a condition for the expression of difference. It is this reciprocity, or the way in which the condition is itself conditioned that distinguishes Deleuze's reciprocal determination from Levinas's argument on the priority of ethics. But doesn't the mathematical definition of continuity and the description of individuals in terms of completeness return us to the possible Levinasian criticisms of Deleuze's higher dialectics? Is there not a sense of a calculus or algorithm in this series of reciprocal determinations?

Method as resistance to system

In order to move closer to an answer to this question, we have to consider the third difference between the two thinkers: their understanding of the possibilities of method. Deleuze's dialectics is based on his ontology. It reflects each part of the structure defined according to the ontology as well as the relations between those parts. His view is that real thought (that is, thought that does not fall into the illusion of an incomplete view of individuals)[53] must comprise critical, transcendental, principled and creative elements. Should it lack any of these it will necessarily fall into illusions concerning the nature of reality. For a complete view of individuals, there must be: a critical study of the illusions of identity and representation; a transcendental search for the conditions for any identity or difference; a principle of completeness governing the search, that is, an endless study of the emergence of identity and search for conditions; a creative destruction, where transgressing experiments seek to go beyond what is already known and to release new sensations.

It is important to note that Deleuze's sense of structure is a very radical version of structuralism where structure is taken to its limit in terms of flexibility and mobility. This comes out very strongly in his 1972 essay on structuralism 'A quoi reconnaît-on le structuralisme?'[54] In the essay, Deleuze redefines structuralism as formal process rather than differential relations between fixed entities. In an analysis of quite familiar aspects of structuralism (the symbolic;

locality or position; the differential and singular; differenciating and differenciation; the serial; empty space; and the move from the subject to practice) he takes each one as depending on differential variations rather than structure. So, for example, locality becomes a locating and dislocating movement rather than a place. Structure then becomes a set of formal distinctions between interconnected processes and Deleuze's method must be understood as a way of responding to these processes rather than a way of setting up relatively fixed structures.

This method responds to the idea that philosophies based purely on the actual or purely on identification miss and suppress virtual pre-conditions for their own arguments. He studies actual sensations in order to deduce these transcendental conditions and he argues that a failure to account for such conditions gives an incomplete view of any actual thing. The virtual and the actual are related to one another and entail changes in one another. So virtual conditions must be turned back on to the actual to investigate their effects and these must then be turned back on to the virtual in an endless process towards a more complete view of both.[55] Deleuze searches for the conditions for each new transcendental condition in order to determine the virtual as fully as possible. To convey the sensual aspect of this relation between the virtual and the actual, he dramatises the role played by the virtual in real thought through an artistic form and through examples from aesthetics. This dramatisation is the creative and destructive aspect of his method; it is destructive due to the necessary selectiveness of the form and examples; some sensations come to the fore while others are relegated into the background.

The stress on the unbreakable relation between critique, transcendental arguments, completeness and experimentation confounds the accusation that this view of method can be reduced to the dominance of 'an ideal necessity'. No part of the method is free of the requirement to experiment and to create openly - into the unknown. However, no part of the method is free from the counter-requirement to experiment from within critique and conditions - from the known. There is neither the totality of a fully conditioned understanding, nor the irresponsibility of a creativity free of an understanding of its presuppositions in representation and identity, and its endless transcendental conditions.

For Deleuze, destructive creation and experimentation are ineluctable aspects of thought. They are about troubling set measures, values and distinctions by opening our senses to the intensities that they presuppose and that make and unmake them: 'Along the broken chain of the tortuous ring we are violently led from the limit of sense to the limit of thought, from what can only be sensed to what can only be thought.'[56] The ring in this passage, that is, the Nietzschean doctrine of eternal return and the challenge of affirming only that which is not the same, is an aspect of Deleuze's method that cannot be eliminated. There can be no algorithm for the affirmation of difference, since only that which resists identification and representation returns. Experimentation is necessary and admits of no recipes or formulae.

So when Levinas describes 'the subject at the service of the system' in *Otherwise than Being or Beyond Essence* his remarks do not apply to Deleuze's structure. Levinas associates relations and structure with intelligibility and signification.[57] This association does not allow the subject to remain independent and open to the face of the other and to ethical responsibility: 'Dissolving into the intelligibility of structures, [the subject] continually sees itself to be at the service of this intelligibility, equivalent to the very appearing of being.'[58] But this cannot apply to Deleuze's structure of virtual and actual, on the contrary, this structure is one that undoes intelligibility through sensation and that calls for experimentation rather than a service to understanding.

When Deleuze speaks of his structure in terms of signs, he calls for signs resistant to an interpretation in terms of a clear meaning. Instead, signs are events associated with that which remains beyond signification and essence, to the point where he insists that sensations are signs of Ideas as inessential events: : 'In this manner, the ground has been superseded by groundlessness, a universal ungrounding which turns upon itself and causes only the yet to come to return.'[59] The infinite as openness is everywhere - free of any hierarchies or restrictions, but requiring complex combinations of critique, enquiry and experimentation.

Notes

1) *Tractatus* 4.1212

2) *Spinoza et le problème de l'expression,* p. 304 [my translation]

3) See, for example, Deleuze's work on Francis Bacon, *Francis Bacon: logique de la sensation,* where Deleuze draws a series of far reaching remarks on the relation between sensation and expression through the concept of rhythm: 'the worlds takes me as myself in closing on me, the self that opens to the world, and open it itself.' *Francis Bacon: logique de la sensation,* p. 31 [my translation]. See also, Deleuze's works on Cinema, *Cinema 1 and 2* : 'In short, expressionism never stops painting the world red on red, one sending us to the terrible non-organic life of things, the other to the sublime non-psychological life of spirit.' *Cinema 1,* p. 81 [my translation].

4) *Difference and Repetition,* p. 260. *Différence et répetition,* p. 334 (Henceforth DR p. xx, p. yy)

5) *Sartre, L'Être et le néant,* p. 349

6) The fundamental reference points for an understanding of Deleuze's view of the individual are Leibniz and the French biologist Simondon. I have discussed the link to the latter in Gilles Deleuze's *Difference and Repetition: a Critical Introduction and Guide,* chapter 7 (See, also, Keith Ansell Pearson's extended work on Deleuze and biology, including Simondon, in *Germinal Life: the Difference and Repetition of Gilles Deleuze.* The reference to the Leibniz is most important in justifying the claim that the individual is an expression of the whole of reality: '... each monad, as individual unity, includes the whole of the series, it thus expresses the whole world, but does not do so without expressing a small region of the world more clearly, a "department", a quarter of the town, a finite sequence.' (Gilles Deleuze, *Le pli: Leibniz et le baroque,* 35 [my translation]) That the Leibnizian monad or Deleuzian individual is an expression of the whole allows both to bypass the paradox of many monads or individuals for the same world, since each expresses the world in a different way, but is included in any other expression. This inclusion is the fold of individuals into each other: '[This definition of the individual suffices] in showing that there is necessarily an infinity of souls and an infinity of points of view, despite the fact that each soul includes and each point of view grasps the infinitely infinite series.' *Le pli: Leibniz et le baroque,* 35 [my translation]

7) See Daniel Smith's discussion of transcendence and immanence in the context of the differences between Deleuze and Derrida. Smith situates Derrida and Levinas as philosophers of transcendence. See 'Deleuze and Derrida: immanence and transcendence' in P. Patton and J. Protevi (eds) *Between Derrida and Deleuze,* pp 43-62.

8) DR 260, 334

9) *Qu'est-ce que la philosophie?,* p. 199 [my translation]

10) An early intimation of this idea emerges in Deleuze's first book, on Hume. Deleuze argues, against brute views of Hume's empiricism, that we must distinguish two senses of empiricism and that neither makes experience constitutive: 'Experience has two senses defined rigorously by Hume, in neither is it constitutive. According to the first, if

we call experience the collection of distinct perceptions, we must recognise that relations do not derive from experience; they are the effect of principles of association...
And, if we deploy the word in its second sense, to designate the diverse conjunctions of
objects in the past, we have to recognise that the principles do not come from experience, on the contrary, experience must be understood as a principle.' Gilles Deleuze,
Empirisme et subjectivité, p. 121. In Deleuze's later works, this becomes the claim that
sensation is constitutive and that it stands as the transcendental condition for both
experience as perception and experience as association or the emergence of identity.

11) Deleuze develops his philosophy of sensation in relation to ethics in terms of the
related concept of intensity in chapter 7 of *Difference and Repetition* and, in a more ethical
context in *Logique du sens*. His argument is that without singular sensations, that is,
without sensations related to intensities beyond measure and beyond compare, we
cannot reach true thought: 'Along the broken chain of the tortuous ring we are violently
led from the limit of sense to the limit of thought, from what can only be sensed to
what can only be thought.' (DR 243, 313) The ethical dimension of this thought is that
if individuals must learn to re-play the events that make them and destroy them as
singular beings, then they must do so by moving with their sensations. Deleuze's ethics
of expression is about becoming an actor for one's own life and about replaying events
in order to stop them falling into truths that elide individuality and destroy free individuals and their creative relation to others: 'That it how the Stoic sage not only
understands and wants the event, but also represents it and thereby selects it, and how
an ethics of miming necessarily prolongs the logics of sense.' *Logique du sens*, p. 173 [my
translation].

12) See Deleuze and Guattari's distinction drawn between percept and perception in
Qu'est-ce que la philosophie? This later use of percept is close to Deleuze's earlier use of
sensation: 'Sensations as percepts are not perceptions that would refer to an object
(reference): if they resemble something, it's a resemblance produced by their own
means, and the smile on the canvas is made only of colours, lines, shade and light.'
(*Qu'est-ce que la philosophie?*, p. 156)

13) Deleuze's most sustained development of these ideas on otherness is in the essay
'Michel Tournier ou le monde sans autrui' in *Logique du sens*. 'The structure Other organ-
ises depth and pacifies it. Makes it livable.' 'Michel Tournier ou le monde sans autrui', p.
366. See also Moira Gatens 'Through a Spinozist lens: ethology, difference, power' in
Deleuze: a Critical Reader.

14) DR 260, 334

15) My thanks go to Lars Iyer, for this important qualification.

16) See Daniel Franco, 'Sur faces: positions du visage chez Lévinas et Deleuze' for an
excellent discussion of the relations between the two thinkers on the face. The essay is
particularly interesting for its work on the relation to Proust in the two philosophers
and for a strong conclusion regarding the differences in the role of explication in their
respective ethics. My thanks go to William Large for this reference and for his invaluable
help in commenting on versions of this paper.

17) *Totality and Infinity*, p. 194. See also Peperzak, *To the Other*, pp 164-5.

18) *Totality and Infinity*, p 193

19) See, John Llewelyn, *Emmanuel Levinas: the Genealogy of Ethics* pp 116-7. Note also
Deleuze's very early interest in the caress in 'Description of woman: for a philosophy of
the sexed other', Trans. K. W. Faulkner, *Angelaki*, Volume 7, Number 3 December 2002,

pp 17-24. I thank Keith Faulkner for this reference.

20) DR 251, 323

21) In *Difference and Repetition*, Deleuze develops the concept of reciprocal determination in the context of his work on Leibniz and differential equations. He then extends the concept to his work on virtual Ideas: 'Ideas always have an element of quantitability, qualitability and potentiality; there are always processes of determinability, of reciprocal determination and complete determination; always distributions of distinctive and ordinary points; always adjunct fields which form the synthetic progression of a sufficient reason.' (DR 181, 235)

22) *Totality and Infinity*, p 198

23) 'Let's not make no mistake about it: what the sadist searches for with such tenacity, what the sadist wants to manipulate and pummel, is the freedom of the Other.' Sartre, *L'Être et le néant*, p. 453.

24) DR 261, 335

25) *Totality and Infinity*, 217

26) DR 182, 235

27) DR 182, 235

28) *Totality and Infinity*, p. 198

29) DR 230, 297; translation slightly modified

30) *Totality and Infinity*, p. 199

31) *Totality and Infinity*, p. 199

32) *Totality and Infinity*, p. 199

33) *Totality and Infinity*, p. 202-3

34) See, John Llewelyn, *Emmanuel Levinas: the Genealogy of Ethics*. 'The infinite is only truly transcendent when the idea of it is always inadequate to it, and the instruction of an absolute Other is necessary to reawaken it.' (p. 98)

35) *Otherwise than Being or Beyond Essence*, p. 149

36) 'Michel Tournier ou le monde sans autrui', p. 360

37) DR 252, 324

38) On the importance of Leibniz's work on the multiple for Deleuze's definition of Ideas, intensity and individuals see his many references to Leibniz's differential calculus, for example, in *Difference and Repetition*, Chapter IV, passim. See also, Deleuze's admiration for Leibniz's discovery of an all-important 'inessential': ''The inessential here refers not to that which lacks importance but, on the contrary, to the most profound, to the universal matter or continuum from which the essences are finally made.' DR 47, 67

39) John Llewelyn, *Emmanuel Levinas: the Genealogy of Ethics*, pp 137-8.

40) This relation to Leibniz is very complicated, since Deleuze is ambivalent in terms of his reception of Leibniz's thought on difference. At times he acknowledges the depth and importance of his thought, for example on infinitesimals or on events, but at others he can be a severe critic: 'Between Leibniz and Hegel it matters little whether the supposed negative of difference is understood as a vice-dicting limitation or a contradicting limitation, any more than it matters whether infinite identity be considered analytic or synthetic. In either case difference remains subordinated to identity, reduced to the negative, incarcerated within similitude or analogy.' (DR 50, 70)

41) DR 162, 210

42) *Totality and Infinity*, p. 200

43) *Totality and Infinity*, p. 201

51

44) *Totality and Infinity*, p. 198

45) *Otherwise than Being or Beyond Essence*, p. 148

46) It is interesting to note the explicit connection between Deleuze and Levinas in thinking about these problems through the opposition of eon or Aeon and chronos, where chronos, or linear time, is seen as conditioned by eternal time or Aeon and as a mistaken subreption or illusion when taken alone (see *The Logic of Sense*, Series 23.

47) *Otherwise than Being or Beyond Essence*, p. 155

48) Jean-François Lyotard, *The Differend* (Manchester University Press, 1988), pp 110-15.

49) DR 38, 56

50) To attempt a critical evaluation of the basis for the ontology would take too much space here and would replicate work I have done elsewhere. See James Williams *Gilles Deleuze's Difference and Repetition: a Critical Introduction and Guide*, esp. Chapters 3, 6 and 7.

51) Deleuze uses Idea with a capital, thereby drawing a strong distinction between Ideas and psychological entities. Instead, Ideas should be thought of in the context of Kantian transcendental ideas of reason, but with great care, since the connection is through their transcendental status and not in terms of their proper definition.

52) DR 182, 236

53) It is important not to confuse Deleuze's concept of completeness with any notion of a final or closed view, in the sense where complete means total. Rather, complete means 'in all its aspects' some of which explicitly bar any possibility of totality or finality.

54) "A quoi reconnaît-on le structuralisme?" in François Châtelet (ed.), *Histoire de la philosophie, t. VIII: le XXeme siècle*, Paris: Hachette, p. 299-335

55) It is important to note the influence of Nietzsche's doctrine of eternal return on Deleuze's elaboration of a structure that does not fall into Levinas's definition of the system. As condition for the sensation of a drive into the new, eternal return cuts the past off from the future (gives time an order). It brings all of time into play because it consigns all identified events to the past and makes all of the future different from all of the past (it conjures up the whole of time). But it only does so when pure differences return, when identity is consigned to the past forever and where there is the sensation of the new free of sameness 'Eternal return affects only the new, what is produced under the condition of absence and by the intermediary of metamorphosis.' DR (90, 122 - translation slightly modified)

56) DR 243, 313

57) *Otherwise than Being or Beyond Essence*, p. 132

58) *Otherwise than Being or Beyond Essence*, p. 133

59) DR 91, 122

4

Deleuze and Bachelard:
completeness and continuity
in dialectics

An Idea is an n-dimensional, continuous, defined multiplicity. (*Gilles Deleuze*, Difference and Repetition, p. 182)

We shall then become aware that continuity is essentially dialectical, that it is the result of a conciliation of contraries and that, temporally, it is made out of rejection, carrying forward into the future, or flowing back to the past. (*Gaston Bachelard*, Dialectique de la durée, 125)

Dialectics

Given Gilles Deleuze's work against Hegelian and post-Hegelian dialectics in *Nietzsche and Philosophy*, it could seem contrary to describe Deleuze's method as dialectics. It could also seem odd to describe his philosophy as a method, given his work on the immediacy of affirmation in the Nietzsche book.[1] However, the term dialectics and new calculus are taken from Deleuze's later work in *Difference and Repetition*, where dialectics take on a positive role and where affirmation and the transcendental become moments in a broader philosophy.[2] Deleuze transforms dialectics by insisting that synthesis is not about reconciling antithetical positions or subsuming oppositions, negations and contradictions. It is about completing a differential reality through syntheses that are at once critical, transcendental and destructively creative.

Here, 'differential reality' means reality understood as a series of differences that are changing through ongoing processes of reciprocal transformation and determination. To seek to complete this reality is to bring as many of these processes together in a creative act that reduces none of them into others. This explains the use of the transcendental in terms of syntheses. Different processes are conditions for one another, that is, an occurrence in one can be seen as presupposing occurrences and forms in another, but without implying a causal relation, or similarities between the occurrences. So the synthesis brings different conditions together, but it cannot conflate them into one another or analyse them according to an external law that holds for all (causality, for instance).

The creation is destructive because it is transformative. According to Deleuze, creation can only take place if identities are sundered and if different processes are selected and highlighted at the expense of others. The synthesis is critical because it involves a diagnosis of the illusory identities that govern the determination of any given set of processes, that is, the actual things that we need to identify and refer to in order to determine or 'get a grip on' ongoing transformations. These are always beyond what we associate with a given perception or concept, but nonetheless they also require them in order to be differentiable from one another. An actual expression or actualisation, in Deleuze's words, is a way of answering the question 'Why this series of processes, rather than that one?' One the other hand, the transcendental move to processes as conditions for actual expressions answers questions such as 'Why are these identities evolving and changing in their significance?'

The incomplete nature of identities explains why their destruction is not a negation or a moment in a negative dialectics. If considered complete, actual identities are illusions. To negate and extend them is to affirm a more connected reality that does not subsume those identities, in the sense of maintaining some effective part of them within a wider and different whole. Instead, only their transcendental conditions pass into new realities. This process will be explained at greater length below, but a key way of understanding it lies in Deleuze's interpretation of Nietzschean eternal return that only pure differences or 'becomings' return eternally rather than identities or 'the same'. This strange claim is a necessary aspect of Deleuze's resistance to primary roles for any sense of identity or negation - for him, the two are inextricably linked - in his metaphysics.

Qualms concerning different definitions of synthesis and dialectics notwithstanding, from the point of view of their methods, Deleuze and Bachelard seem to have much in common. Both choose to name their methods 'dialectics' in opposition to Cartesianism. Both stress the importance of the concepts of synthesis and completeness in dialectics. They share common intuitions as to why we should move away from the Cartesian rationalism of analysis and deduction. In addition, they share the view that reality is unavoidably and valuably complex.

These intuitions also involve a suspicion of brute objectivity, of crude empiricism and of basic metaphysical or scientific notions resistant to further differentiation. In characterising their dialectics, both resort to mathematics. They experiment with the idea of dialectics as a new, anti-Cartesian and irregular *mathesis universalis*. This is based on the evolution of mathematics through the adjunction of new theories, in the case of Bachelard. It is based on the role of the adjunction of differentials and integrations in calculus, in the case of Deleuze.

Having developed their dialectics, both thinkers lay great stress on the concept of rhythm. It allows them to account the development and determinacy of their dialectics in practical contexts. For example, Deleuze depends on the concept in his account of the importance of refrains and ritornellos in *A Thousand Plateaus* or in his account of harmony and 'concertation' in the Baroque in *The Fold: Leibniz and the Baroque*. Towards the end of *La dialectique de la durée*, Bachelard depends on rhythm to connect the intellectual and spiritual sides of life in a coherent, but not a reductive whole: 'Poetry, thus liberated from habitual training, became a model for rhymed life and thought. It was thus the most proper way to rhythm-analyse spiritual life and to return the dialectics of duration to the mastery of spirit.'[3] The same rhymed resistance to a reduction of many lines to a single one is also described by Deleuze: 'These lines do not disappear, obviously, but they do submit to a harmonic principle.'[4]

Priorities and contexts

However, from these striking surface similarities, Deleuze and Bachelard diverge profoundly and with interesting critical oppositions. This divergence takes place around the characterisation of their dialectics through the relations holding between the concepts of completeness and continuity. Again, both thinkers lay great weight on the latter concept but with utterly different definitions and valuations. More precisely, the priority given to continuity in dialectics relating continuity and discontinuity is the key to understanding the difference between the two. For Deleuze, continuity is prior from the point of view of evolution, change, creation and relations to the future. This is because a form of ideal continuity is the condition for the transgression of actual discontinuous boundaries, in individuals, species, persons, subjects. For Bachelard, it is exactly the opposite. Discontinuity explains the possibility of breaking with continuous series and beginning new ones that cannot share the same premises or axioms as the first.

Different views of the priority to be given to continuity and discontinuity lead to opposed definitions of synthesis in relation to the new in dialectics. In turn, this leads to different definitions of completeness. For Bachelard, completeness is a matter of holding together discontinuities. For Deleuze, it is a matter of drawing out the continuities underlying discontinuities. For both, though, the question of completeness turns on the new, both in terms of historical novelty and relations to the future. The question 'How radical is the new?' is answered in different ways by Deleuze and Bachelard due to their disagreements about continuity and about how this impacts on the concept of completeness. Neither believes that the new cannot be assimilated in any way, nor do they think that it can be completely assimilated. Instead, the difference lies in questions concerning how thought comes to work with the new in the context of a dialectics.

Bachelard constructs a dialectics around the problem of how to think methodologically given a demand for completeness and a lack of continuity. He is responding to the challenge of adding the new to that which is already relatively known, whilst accepting that there can be no final perfect fit between them. Reality is essentially discontinuous, but thought can bridge this discontinuity through the synthetic transformations and implicit relativity of dialectics. The status of propositions changes through successive adjunctions. There are no ultimate truths that are not open to revision after experimentation.

Deleuze constructs his dialectics around the problem of how to affirm a productive continuity through a search for completeness, whilst also responding to the proposition that continuity is never a matter of identities or representations. In other words, we can never represent or identify continuity, even relatively and in an open-ended transforming way. Yet reality is continuous and it is possible to speak of better or worse affirmations of that continuity in accordance with individual problems. This is the paradoxical challenge of his dialectics. Though, here, paradox must be given a positive sense, since Deleuze takes paradoxes as paradigms for the relation of continuity and discontinuity: continuous connected conditions hold together discontinuous contradictories. This concession to Deleuze should be made carefully, though, since if he is wrong about this conditioning, he is also wrong about paradoxes.

There are two contextual contrasts that are helpful in reaching an understanding of the divergence of the two thinkers. First, Bachelard and Deleuze arrive at their dialectics through very different subject matter. Deleuze shares some of Bachelard's interest in science and mathematics. Bachelard is interested in the historical and metaphysical roots of the need for dialectics. Yet the former is responding, first and foremost, to the problem of the negative power of metaphysics that are based on representations and transcendence.

Whilst the latter is responding, first and foremost, to the problem of scientific completeness in the light of scientific developments - at least in his early work (the later work will be considered in the next point). It could be said that Bachelard is closer to the early Whitehead of *Science and the Modern World*[5] - where philosophy comes in after a survey of history and science. Whereas Deleuze is closer to the later *Process and Reality*[6]- where speculative philosophy and metaphysical creativity retain an independence from the observation of science and the history of science. This is a matter of emphasis, rather than total opposition. It is significant, though, because Deleuze is concerned with questions of how metaphysics came to foster the illusion of foundational and transcendent identities and of how to draw out the virtual and continuous conditions for these illusions. Bachelard, on the other hand, is concerned with questions about the philosophical lessons to be learnt from the breaks implied by scientific discoveries, both in terms of philosophy of science, but also in terms of epistemology and ontology.

This relation to science as point of evidence for philosophy is all-important in understanding the Deleuze-Bachelard opposition. Yet, it is also one of the most delicate problems in interpreting their philosophies. For example, Manuel DeLanda, in his *Intensive Science and Virtual Philosophy*,[7] and John Protevi, in his *Political Physics* have recently proposed strongly science-based readings of Deleuze. These are greatly at odds with the premises that underlie this essay.[8] What I hope to show in this chapter is that, for all its strengths, this science-based reading is a limitation on the radical nature of the new and of the future in Deleuze's philosophy. This is because it ties Deleuze to a given scientific theory and thereby opens him up to a critique based on Bachelard's understanding of historical breaks in science. Deleuze shares a concern with these breaks and with their future necessity or possibility (necessary, for Deleuze; possible, for Bachelard). For both, philosophy cannot have an apodictic ground in mathematics and science because that ground has shifted and may continue to shift. Instead, it is a matter of mathematics informing and providing models and examples for philosophy, but with philosophy retaining an extra-scientific form of thought.

Bachelard assigns great importance to philosophical intersections with the history of science and the emergence of scientific theories, for example, in his attacks on Cartesian epistemologies. My claim, though, is that scientific developments, rather than their historical philosophical consequences, are the main drivers behind the emergence of his dialectics and the problems he is responding to. Whereas, for Deleuze, problems always have strongly philosophical roots. This difference can be seen, for example, in their treatment of

Descartes, where the former is particularly interested in Cartesian epistemology in the light of modern science,[9] whereas the latter is more interested in the contrast between Cartesian analysis and a concept of synthesis coming out of Spinoza or the idea of the transcendental coming out of Kant and its relations to Bergson's and to Nietzsche's philosophies.[10]

The second contrast, helpful for an understanding of the differences between Deleuze and Bachelard, lies in the philosophical methods adopted as ways into 'the given', prior to further work in terms of dialectics (I use the term given here in order not to prejudge the differences at play through terms such as phenomena, facts or intuitions). These methods are an important part of the dialectics, they provide the starting point where the structure and basic content of the dialectics are mapped out - though in a way that is necessarily open to revision. Thus, these prior methods are not independent of the dialectics. They are fully part of them, but an important part, since they provide the actual material for the broader method to work on.

In his works on philosophy, science and art, Bachelard gives great weight to phenomenology taken from a wide range of sources. In contrast, Deleuze emphasizes a new way of developing transcendental philosophy (see the chapter on Deleuze and Kant, here). Furthermore, where Bachelard takes the mind and psychology as key starting points, Deleuze takes sensibility and the affects, as expressed through the arts and defined, among others, by Nietzsche and Spinoza. Deleuze is explicitly critical of phenomenology, particularly in its Sartrean guise. Bachelard is particularly critical of transcendental moves, particularly in their Bergsonian guise.[11]

Anti-Cartesian dialectics

In his introduction to *Le nouvel esprit scientifique*, Bachelard sets out a philosophical programme responding to the scientific discoveries of the late Nineteenth and early Twentieth centuries. His main argument is that a new scientific spirit demands changes in philosophical views of reality and method: 'Sooner or later, scientific thought will become the fundamental theme of philosophical polemics; this thought will lead intuitive and immediate metaphysics to be substituted by objectively rectified discursive metaphysics.' (NES, 6) Philosophy will become a dialectical method that privileges objective scientific discoveries.

However, it is very important to realise that, by objective rectification, Bachelard does not mean a direct response or reflection on pure facts or data. On the contrary, objective rectification is already a scientific dialectics, where theories are always part of an ongoing debate around new discoveries, to the point where there are no pure objective facts: 'If immediate reality is only a simple pretext of scientific thought and no longer an object of knowledge, we shall have to pass from the *how* of description to theoretical *commentary*.' (NES, 10) Thus truth becomes not a matter of objectivity, but of debate: 'Every new truth is born despite the evidence, every new experience is born despite immediate experience.' (NES, 11)

There are therefore no straightforward propositional correspondences to evidence or to facts. Scientific propositions take place within a series of conditions that define and determine what is to count as a fact in relation to other claims about evidence. For example, there is a contrast between commonsensical or deeply ingrained suppositions about the nature of matter and definitions that emerge from modern physics. What is to be looked for and what is to count as a significant empirical result is partly a result of debates between these positions.

In making these points about truth, Bachelard shows a further point of connection with Deleuze and with the preparation for Deleuze's mature philosophy. The notion of a truth 'despite' fact and experience is related to Nietzsche's counter-intuitive definition of truth: 'As Nietzsche says: everything that is decisive is only born *despite*.' (NES, 11) Yet, this connection to Nietzsche on truth is a narrow one. In the philosophy-science relation, Bachelard still privileges science and the debate between rationalism and realism in science: 'In effect, science creates philosophy. The philosopher must inflect his language in order to translate contemporary thought in its suppleness and mobility.' (NES, 7) It is not so much that Nietzsche does not value science - he does. Rather, it is that science takes its place in a very wide set of metaphysical claims according to Deleuze's reading of Nietzsche (eternal return, for example). This is not the case in Bachelard's reading: in fact, it is a position he is explicitly trying to move beyond.

For him, modern science demands a dialectical position between theory and fact, indeed, between theories, facts and further theories. This demand is born of necessity. There is no pure theory (*pace* Descartes and Kant). There are no pure facts (*pace* Russell) or even, in a more up-to-date form, irreducible properties such as qualia.[12] So any scientific theory is necessarily dialectical, not only between fact and theory, but between different theoretical assumptions about different facts.

Bachelard is then quick to insist that this dialectics is not one of opposition. It is not that facts contradict theories, neither is it that theories straightforwardly contradict one another. Rather, the nature of the debate is a two-directional one. Facts only appear thanks to theories, notably, on how to simplify reality so that it may reveal facts. Theories make claims about reality that are undermined by the complexity revealed by scientific discovery. There is a dialectics between the need to simplify and the discovery of complexity.

This is not a nihilistic relativism where disbelief in facts and in explanations leads to a questioning of all knowledge. Bachelard gives precise descriptions of his dialectics and of a relativism associated with progress and projects, rather than with the danger of some generalised doubt: 'In fact, as soon as the object is presented as a complex of relations, it must be apprehended through multiple methods. Objectivity cannot be separated from the social character of the task. We can only arrive at objectivity by exposing a method of objectification in a discursive and detailed way.' (NES, 16) So it is not that we cannot tend towards objectivity - with all the possible positive judgements regarding progress and certainty about error and truth that this entails. Rather, it is that we never have absolute facts or final theories immune from new facts.

Bachelard thinks that this detailed and precise form of dialectics and sense of arriving at objectivity can only come from science (NES, 18). Moreover, it is as a model of a psychological process that science stands out. This psychology is not one of negation or opposition, but one of synthesis in terms of rectification and precision: '... an empirical rectification is joined to a theoretical precision.' (NES, 19) Modern science teaches us that theories are rectified and added to through new empirical discoveries. The techniques surrounding experiments and the things tested-for are made more precise in the light of theory.

Psychologically, modern science does not evolve through the discarding of theories through contradictions with new theories or simple falsification, rather, theories have to be included in greater and sometimes looser collections of theories. These have the aim of seeking greater cohesion, but not through simplifications:

> Thus it seems to us that truly new epistemological principles must be introduced into contemporary scientific philosophy. Once such principle, for example, would be the idea that complementary characters must be inscribed in the essence of being, thus breaking with that tacit belief that being is always the sign of unity. Indeed, if being in itself is a principle that is communicated to the mind - in the same way as a material point enters in relation with a field of action - it could not be a symbol of unity. We should therefore found an ontology of the complementary less harshly dialectical than the metaphysics of the contradictory. (NES, 20)

Setting aside, for a while, the strong connection to Deleuze on being as becoming and multiplicity and the strong difference with his work insofar as Bachelard's points are expressed in terms of a psychology, this important passage highlights three important aspects of Bachelard's dialectics. We should seek completeness through the addition of complementary theories. Complementary does not mean fully unified. Neither does it mean contradictory.

These aspects become more clear in the final chapter of *Le nouvel esprit scientifique* on non-Cartesian epistemology. First, like Deleuze's work on biology and thermodynamics in *Difference and Repetition*, Bachelard is concerned with the way modern science can complicate our experience of the world in addition to explaining it.[13] Where Descartes seeks simplifications with great explanatory power, Bachelard sees the emergence of the idea of an 'essential complexity of elementary phenomena' (NES, 143). These cannot be reduced legitimately and methodologies that do so must be mistaken. There has to be a dialectics between complexity and explanation. Where the latter seeks to eliminate contradictions and to arrive at unity, the former allows contradictory positions to complement one another in order to arrive at a richer objective view or relation between fact and theory.

Deleuze tempers this positive view of complication with the observation that all sciences must necessarily have an explanatory side that extends into a denial of radical complication or complexity. So, in contrast to Bachelard, Deleuze refuses the interpretation of modern sciences as going beyond explanation in the dialectical privileging of complication through theory. Instead, the desire for completeness is already a sign of an explanatory simplification of the richness of a prior intensity (this term will be defined more fully below). For Deleuze, a scientific definition of complication could already be part of an explanatory process that restricted a prior metaphysical openness.

In emphasising complication over explanation, it is not that Bachelard ignores the pedagogical side of modern science - quite the contrary. It is that he situates pedagogy after discovery, as if the simplification demanded by it remains at arms length from discovery proper. Whereas Deleuze sees explanation as a necessary betrayal of complexity, even in the most pure moments of scientific advance. The problem of explanation is not pedagogical, but proper to scientific method. Thus Deleuze situates learning at the core of his philosophy and dialectics can be seen as a creative and experimental learning process. From this point of view, Bachelard's discussion of pedagogy shows a mistaken view of the nature of teaching and learning and of its relative position with respect to discovery.

Bachelard analyses the flaws in Cartesian methodology in terms of identity: '[contemporary scientific] thought tries to find pluralism beneath identity, to imagine occasions for breaking with identity, beyond immediate experience summed up too quickly as the aspect of a group.' (NES, 143) This could have led him to see a tendency to deny complexity in modern science too, in the connections to Cartesian theory in modern science (philosophy of mind and epistemology, for example).[14] But Bachelard concentrates on those aspects of science that strike against Cartesian tendencies. Deleuze is more attuned to the capacity of those tendencies to arise anew and to lie in wait in even the most apparently open and pluralist sciences. This difference in degrees of 'optimism' with respect to the fall of Cartesianism is reflected in the way in which each dialectics is posited on progress. With Bachelard, a scientifically guided dialectics is necessarily progressive. With Deleuze, a dialectics is a struggle with the power of identity to cover multiplicity because they determine one another (always and forever).

For Deleuze, any thought (and not just Cartesianism) must combine a creative complexity and explanatory simplification - a folding and unfolding of reality. This is because reality is always a relation between a continuity that undermines and transforms identity and a discontinuity that allows the open plurality of continuous ideas to be determined. Any scientific advance must therefore have a dual quality and the role of the philosopher is to comment on and work with both, whilst resisting ideas that make final claims for either one (*We finally have the simple theory that accounts for all events. All explanations are but illusory accounts of order against the original nonsense and futility of life*).

Yet Bachelard does not see this temptation as implied by modern science. Partly, this is because he defines synthesis in modern science in terms of a priori mathematical syntheses: not as a move to find objective unity, but as a way of bringing together an objective plurality through the way mathematics bring complementary fields together without reducing them to one-another (his main examples for this are the relation between Euclidean and Non-Euclidean mathematics and their relation to Newtonian physics and the physics of relativity). According to Bachelard, mathematical synthesis resolves problems, but also raises new questions and introduces new fields. Its synthetic value is productive rather than reductive. It is worth noting that Deleuze makes much of a similar non-reductive nature of intensity in relations between different number theories (DR, 234).

Mathematical synthesis sheds results by adding fields, but does not depend on presumptions of a prior identity: 'That mathematical description is not clear through its elements. It is only clear in its achievement through a sort of consciousness of its synthetic value... all basic notions can in some way be doubled; they can be bordered by complementary notions.' (NES, 146) For Bachelard, mathematics progress through new perspectives, rather than being pushed forward by a single dominant one. Complementary notions allow for connections that split basic elements and look at them in new ways. We still have the same elements or basic notions, but expanded into different branches that are related yet not the same. The productive and synthetic quality of this relation provides us with a model for a progressive rational dialogue across differences.

His dialectics then becomes the questioning search for 'variations under identity' that 'shed light on the first thought by completing.' (NES, 150) This is not, then, a structure of scientific revolutions. It is a structure of scientific additions and revisions, where each addition involves changes in the objective status of what it adds to. This is shown in a very beautiful passage on laws: 'We shall not speak of simple laws that are then disrupted, but of complex and organic laws touched sometimes by certain viscosities, certain obliterations. The old simple law becomes a simple example, a mutilated truth, the beginnings of an image, a sketch on a board.' (NES, 161) A law can be thought-of as a living organic thing in a symbiotic relation with others and other realms of life. It has ages, evolutions, injuries and death (where it survives only as a pedagogical skeleton).

Doubt at all levels, perfectibility and rectifiable properties become the principles for Bachelard's dialectics, as it moves towards a progressive objectification free of any final subjectivity, simple law and metaphysical ground. Here we begin to glimpse the great rift with Deleuze. Against the notion of historical eternal return - that is of simple repeated historical cycles - Bachelard speaks of 'thoughts that do not begin again; these are thoughts that have been rectified, enlarged, completed.' (NES, 177) We shall see that Deleuze depends on a counter-notion of the possibility of eternal return that depends on a notion of continuity underlying actual discontinuity.

Bachelard has to posit a prior discontinuity, thereby ensuring that differences can only be bridged partially. This is because he needs to explain how past thoughts remain an active part of our present ones, instead of disappearing totally in new and hermetic theories that owe nothing to the past (except as what they have gone beyond, destroyed and escaped). The past and the present are only completed, never complete:

> ... would it not be right, in order to understand intellectual evolution, to pay attention to anxious thought, to thought in search of an object, to thought looking for dialectical occasions for going beyond itself, to break with its frames, in short, a thought on the way to objectification. (NES, 181)

Continuity and discontinuity

Deleuze's dialectics differ from the above account of Bachelard's in at least two major ways. First, Deleuze denies the possibility of progress as defined by Bachelard in *Le nouvel esprit scientifique*. For Deleuze, there can be actual progress, but this must be set against the eternal return of difference, that is, the significance of actual progress changes in terms of the eternal and necessary return of intensities, virtual Ideas and sensations, where these can be given a first, simple, definition as indicators of significance or value resistant to our understanding of actual processes (DR, 297). Established ways of explaining, understanding and judging the world are vulnerable to new ways of feeling and thinking about it.

So it is perfectly possible to speak of scientific progress, but it is not possible to assign any independence to that progress with respect to value and to sensibility. This is important from the point of view of Bachelard's modelling of philosophical dialectics on scientific dialectics and from the point of view of his dependence on science and phenomenology for philosophical material. Philosophy cannot be simply progressive in the same way as science.

Furthermore, it is possible to provide a Deleuzian argument against the specificity of scientific invention - situating it instead as a case of a wider form of creativity. Creative thought does not have science as its principal model, instead, many different forms of thought create and evolve through combinations of new ideas, sensations and intensities. From the point of view of this definition of creativity, as open selection through sensibility, intensity and the expression of Ideas, Bachelard gives an overly negative and programmatic account of creativity in the sciences. He may therefore have also given a mistaken account of dialectics based on a restrictive account of the 'psychology' of the scientist.

The second key point to be made by Deleuze against Bachelard concerns continuity. Where Bachelard claims that dialectics is a matter of the search for completeness through discontinuous but not opposed terms. Deleuze argues that beneath every actual difference, beneath every disparity, lies a continuous transcendental condition for actual difference, where actual difference is defined in terms of identity. In *Difference and Repetition*, this argument is developed in terms of pure differences underlying measured spaces (DR, 229). He claims that any measuring is a restriction of prior immeasurable intensities that explain how there can be changes in measurement and why measurement is never the last word on the significance of what it measures.

These points are linked, since, when Deleuze speaks of the eternal return of difference, he means the return of the expression of continuous virtual Ideas and intensities. These return under different configurations or perplications (envelopments), in the case of intensities, and different relations of distinctness and obscurity, in the case of transcendental Ideas. For Deleuze, there is no possibility of discontinuity between intensities and between Ideas; such breaks only appear when they are actually expressed. Even then, a complete expression must always take account of the connection of all actual things through the virtual:

> [...] all the intensities are implicated in one another, each in turn enveloped and enveloping, such that each continues to express the changing totality of Ideas, the variable ensemble of differential relations. However, each intensity clearly expresses only certain relations or certain degrees of variation. Those that it expresses *clearly* are precisely those on which it is focused when it has the *enveloping* role. In its role as the enveloped, it still expresses all relations and all degrees, but *confusedly*. As the two roles are reciprocal, and as intensity is in the first instance enveloped by itself, it must be said that the clear and the confused, as logical characteristics in the intensity which expresses the idea - in other words, in the individual which thinks it - are no more separable than the distinct and the obscure are separable in the Idea itself. (DR, 252)

Underlying actual things and standing as transcendental conditions for their variation, we find intensities and Ideas that cannot be finally separated from one another, because such separation would introduce illegitimate limits in the conditioned realm of actual things. There is no grounds for introducing an arbitrary set of final distinctions in processes that evolve in contact with one another. On the contrary, that evolution and the irruption of new events that break distinctions that we assumed to be final presupposes a condition for connection and differences that resist identification. So Ideas and intensities can only be determined as separate according to degrees and according to relations of distinctness and obscurity, where distinctness only appears with a wider varying set of more or less obscure relations.

Bachelard's counter to such claims is developed in *La dialectique de la durée*. It is constructed around the thesis that psychology and phenomenology of time imply discontinuity. This discontinuity of time implies an ontological discontinuity. Every continuity is therefore illusory and, in fact, secondary with respect to a dialectics that comes out of the possibility of affirmation or negation in activity: 'To think is to abstract certain experiences, it is to plunge them into the shadow of nothingness. If one objected to us that these effaced positive experience subsist nonetheless, we would answer that they subsist without playing a role in our actual knowledge.' (DD, 16) Because we make negative judgements we have to suppose that reality is discontinuous, in the sense of allowing gaps or empty space and time in existence.

For Deleuze, this is to miss the role of passive syntheses as transcendental conditions for activity. These conditions imply a continuity at the level of Ideas and a complicated continuity at the level of time. But a further rejoinder can be found in Bachelard's response to the question of the transcendental:

> We believe that we must give ourselves a little more than simple temporal possibility characterised as an *a priori* form. We must give ourselves the temporal alternative analysed through these two verifications: either in this instant nothing is happening, or in this instant something is happening. Time is therefore continuous as possibility, as nothingness. It is discontinuous as being. In other words, we start with a temporal duality and not a unity. We rest that duality on function, rather than on being. (DD, 25)

Time as condition must be discontinuous, given the nature of our consciousness of things as having the potential to exist or not. There is a discontinuity between these two states and Bachelard will go on to argue that this discontinuity is replicated in consciousness through our power to negate and to make decisions between different possible routes.

Syntheses of time: Deleuze's critique of discontinuity

The opposition around continuity described above can be summed up through two opposed arguments. Deleuze's line is that actual events presuppose a transcendental continuity, because such events cannot simply be accounted for in terms of identities. Identities are encountered in events that vary according to a 'drama' of multiple sensations and hence intensities. For example, there is no finally isolated moment of decision in psychology, only the awareness of deciding or of signs of a decision, abstracted from endless and variegated rises and falls in tension in feelings and processes. The abstraction can make us think that time is essentially discontinuous, in the sense of thinking 'Everything changed here, at this point.' But the break is always changing in significance according to the variations that surround it (in a declaration and its context, for example).

For Bachelard, on the other hand, the argument goes that science and phenomenology are the only proper sources of evidence for conclusions concerning time. What they show is that we have to assume that time is discontinuous, in order to account for the psychology of decisions and choices, and for the phenomenology of intentionality. Were time continuous, then our sense of points of decision, of breaks where events could go one way or another, would be mistaken. All the evidence points to the contrary. Our experiences are of discontinuous events, where things stop and start, where they can be made to stop and start, and where our directedness to events presupposes such breaks. The fact of negation, where we can stop things, or where things stop, or where our directedness implies the necessity of stops and starts, shows that time must be discontinuous.

In reply, we can look at a scientifically isolated point of decision (or at least sign of such) 'The rat moves to A' or 'The mapping of brain patterns changes dramatically at this point'. From a Deleuzian point of view, each isolation is open to re-examination according to wider patterns of significance, that is, according to different flows of sensations and of the problems that surround them. In other words, the scientific or phenomenological point will move. It may even be located at plural points, or according to neighbourhoods or stretches that deny the importance of a single point.

But this shift to relative plurality is not the issue for Deleuze. Rather, it is what the shift presupposes that bothers him - not what it leads to. Why did we change our view of what stands as the point of decision? Can that change be explained in purely scientific terms (new discoveries) or phenomenological terms (different and more complex views of intentionality)? Or, rather, do we have to look further in terms of why we continue to search for changes in a given direction? Shouldn't we look at why that direction changes and at why we view the results of that change in different and perhaps ultimately individual ways?

Deleuze's transcendental deductions around three syntheses of time point to conditions for discontinuity that are themselves continuous. An active decision presupposes all the repetitions and variations that have come together into forming a being capable of making the decision. Indeed, even the short-hand of 'being' or 'actor' is insufficient. What we should say is that a given situation, comprising a decision and its environment, has no limit in principle with respect to the extent of the environment and actor in terms of antecedents (DR, 77). It is possible to say that an ancestry 'decides' or that the decision lies in the relation between a climate and that ancestry. It is not possible to say that any point of that ancestry or environment is excluded in principle.

67

Furthermore, actual repetitions that lead to a decision have to be extended into a field of virtual memory (Bergson's pure past). It is not only the hard-wired aspects of the past that matter, but also soft and highly variable virtual ones (DR, 81-2). This is something that Deleuze shows in his work on cinema. Our memory is a swirling and changeable record of the past. Yet it is played out in present acts. Again, no limitation in principle makes sense. More seriously, there cannot even be a linear limitation, as might have been thought in the actual repetitions (*This must have happened first*). Memory can be re-jigged in the present, to the point where we have to say that we act on the virtual past and also, therefore, on the relation of that virtual past to actual past repetitions. Equally, though, the virtual past acts on us, thereby setting off relations of reciprocal determination of memory and actuality.[15]

For instance, the realisation of a betrayal changes our memories and colours them in different ways (*He was stealing money all that time*). That new past changes the relation of our current acts to their preparation, in the sense that different repetitions, environments and skills come to the fore, whilst other recede (*I shall make him pay here and like this*). A skilful filmmaker exploits this property of time and memory, changing our sense of the film as a whole as it unfolds through new disclosures and concealments. This does not have to be restricted to art-house films; arguably, any thriller exploits this property, for example, in the uncertainty around Keyser Soze in *The Usual Suspects*,[16] where the whole film changes in the final shots.

But does any of this work on memory imply continuity? Should we still not speak of actual identifiable things in repetitions and environments? Should we not do the same with respect to memories? Everything may have to be thought of in limitless chains. This may force us to accept the necessity of contingent abstractions. But that does not mean that such abstractions do not take place in essentially discontinuous realms. From Bachelard's point of view, what matters is that I have had to refer to the end of the film and it is this identifiable moment that changes a series of earlier discontinuous points. The film drives a desire to find out, that is, to reach a point that resolves tensions in earlier ones. Were all things continuous that drive could not be explained, since we would not have the final point and its capacity to organise time around it.

To answer these questions we have to go beyond Deleuze's first two syntheses of time ('Every present event presupposes syntheses of actual chains of repetitions.' and 'Every present act presupposes the synthesis of the whole of the virtual past.') However, prior to that, it is important to make a point concerning the relations that hold between all three of Deleuze's syntheses. Each one is incomplete without the others - they presuppose one another. We have already seen that the first synthesis and the second are connected and cannot be separated. This is because actual repetitions and acts take place and acquire significance with virtual memory. This is as true for a material or biological process as it is for a conscious being.

Deleuze's point is that the synthesis of the pure virtual past is a necessary condition for the synthesis of an active present: 'There is thus a substantial temporal element (the Past which was never present) playing the role of ground.' (DR, 82) That ground is what allows an act in the present to be determined in terms of how it rearranges the whole of the past and hence also in terms of how it acquires significance, determinacy and value in relation to the present: '... if the new present is always endowed with a supplementary dimension, this is because it is reflected in the element of the pure past in general, whereas it is only *through* this element that we focus upon the former present as a particular.' (DR, 82) The present is incomplete unless is considered in relation to all the things it passes away into (the pure past).

When a chalk cliff suddenly loses a large section, thereby changing a landscape, the large-scale event presupposes repetitions of storms, tides, formation of rocks. Each of these synthesises its own cycles, where what matters is the variation in any repetition, that is, what changes each time, and not what remains the same. But why should any of this refer to virtual memory? The answer is in the selection of the event and of the pathways of repetitions. What happens when a particular event is isolated? How is it isolated? The material selection presupposes an ideal one, in the sense where the record of the past is re-written through the selection and in the sense where that re-writing is a condition for the material selection.

It is possible to think of this interdependence in terms of value. Seen as brute material processes, chains of repetitions are neutral with respect to value (Why celebrate the birth of an animal? Shrug at the erosion of a rock? Ignore a microscopic change?) When events are selected, value impinges to introduce hierarchies. But what is this value? For Deleuze, it is itself a selection through sensations and these depend on past associations of ideas and sensations. There is therefore a virtual, immaterial, trace of selections that runs through all of the virtual past and this trace introduces value and selection into actual processes. There is a virtual history of value that allows for determinations in the actual. Why did you care so about that rock face? What selections did that care imply?

This reference to selection as the appearance of the new in an unfolding series of events is at the core of both Deleuze's and Bachelard's arguments. For Deleuze, selection implies a third synthesis of time as a relation to the future. This synthesis implies continuity in all syntheses and through all things. A continuous relation - that Deleuze will define in terms of intensities and virtual Ideas - is presupposed by all actual events. For Bachelard, as we shall see in detail in the next section, it is quite the opposite: selection and the new presuppose discontinuity.

Deleuze's argument is that selection, as the drive towards the new, presupposes a cut, assembly and transformation of all of time. The first point is not controversial, at least in this context, since it supports Bachelard's point. To select the new, we presuppose that it cuts away from the past in some way. The next point is that though there is a cut, it is one that takes place with the backdrop of the past. Therefore, the cut projects that past into the future. A decision or an unconscious selection does not only cut away from the past, it brings something new into the past and brings the past into the future. So though there is a break, there is also an assembly. A discontinuous and continuous time are implied by selection.

For example, the decision to move to a new kind of experiment or to a new way of living or form of behaviour shears off from the past and attempts something untried and original. But, in terms of the production of memory or of the past and in terms of earlier chains of repetitions, the experiment and the new form bring them into play in the future. So selection is a cut and an assembly of the past and the future. But isn't this a contradiction? How can time be both continuous and discontinuous? Is it not rather the case that time is discontinuous throughout and that Deleuze's assembly is an assembly of prior cuts and later ones?

His answer lies in the third property of selection. The assembly of the past and the future are transformations of them. So it is possible to speak of a cut and of an assembly, because the assembly is of different things. When thinking of the future (F) as different from the past (P), we may be tempted to think that the difference lies between P and F. But Deleuze's point is that in a selection we move from an assembly P/F to a new assembly P'/F'. We select a new past and a new future. So any difference is between P/F and P'/F'. However, isn't this even more nonsensical than the previous contradiction? How can we change the past and the future in the present?

In *Difference and Repetition*, Deleuze's answer is usually couched in terms of Nietzsche's doctrine of eternal return, but I want to give a different version that links more easily to his ideas about intensities and virtual Ideas. It is the case that any given actual identical thing cannot return, what returns are pure differences and what changes is the relation of these to actual things. When we spoke of the pure past and of virtual Ideas and intensities earlier, these could have been understood as identifiable memories - open to representation. For Deleuze, the virtual is the transcendental condition for transformations, that is, for the sensations that something is actually different though in an unidentifiable way (if it could be identified, then it would not be new in the sense of implying a cut.)

These conditions are always defined as continuous for Deleuze. Otherwise, forms of identity and representation would return in the virtual, thereby contradicting his argument that the new must be radical in the sense of departing from the present and from the past, whilst transforming them: 'The synthesis of time here constitutes a future which affirms at once both the unconditioned character of the product in relation to the conditions of its production, and the independence of the work in relation to its author or actor.' (DR, 94)

For this unconditioned character to hold, and yet for there to be an assembly and transformation of the conditions of production, the new presupposes something that escapes both the actor and the production (past and present). This is the transcendental field of the virtual. The radical nature of the new as expressed through sensations implies therefore that this field must be continuous - and hence independent of actor and production, in the sense of in principle unidentifiable in terms of them. It must change only as continuous, that is, in terms of relations of distinctness and obscurity, rather than in terms of relation of opposition and identity.

The transcendental field is a continuous multiplicity of varying relations that stands as the condition for the new as cut and transformation, for example, as condition for the fractured I and dissolved self: 'As we have seen, what swarms around the edges of the fracture are Ideas in the form of problems - in other words, in the form of multiplicities made up of differential relations and variations of relations, distinctive points and transformations of points.' (DR, 259). For Deleuze, the new presupposes continuity, otherwise, we could not explain its novelty.

Bachelard's arguments against continuity

Bachelard puts forward many different arguments against the continuity of time in his critique of Bergson in *La dialectique de la durée*: 'We should like to develop an essay of discontinuous Bergsonism, in showing the necessity to arithmetise Bergsonian duration in order to give it greater fluidity, more numbers, greater exactitude too in the correspondence that holds between phenomena of thought and the quantic qualities of the real.' (DD, 8) Given Deleuze's dependence on Bergson for key arguments about time, in particular, in terms of his second synthesis of time, and given the strong Bergsonian influence on Deleuze, it is no surprise that many of Bachelard's arguments also apply to Deleuze.

In most of his works, Bachelard's method involves a close and up-to-date study of different scientific findings relevant to his topic. In other words, he takes his own dialectics very seriously in its situating of philosophy with, but also after, science. Philosophy is a discipline that learns from scientific advances and that contributes to the evolution of science as a rational pursuit guided by a dialectical approach to the relation of theory to objective scientific discoveries and vice-versa. That's why the passage above highlights the correspondence between a scientific approach to the real and a phenomenological approach to thought. There is an ongoing debate and accommodation between experience and discovery.

This approach to science as starting point for reflection is problematic. First, the two thinkers are not dealing with the same science, including mathematics. Second, Bachelard's studies far outreach Deleuze's work. The former works on primary and often cutting edge sources (the latest theorems in mathematical journals in his exemplary study of Adolphe Buhl's work in *La Philosophie du non*, for instance).[17] The latter tends to work on philosophical digests of such work, or on broader primary sources and in a much less detailed scientific manner, but perhaps with a greater sense of the intricacies of philosophical ontological arguments in their relation to science. Bachelard is a mathematician and a philosopher of science. He is attempting to bring philosophy up to the level of the scientific discoveries of his age.[18] Deleuze is a metaphysician whose system seeks to develop a coherent account of science within a wider metaphysics.

So, for Bachelard, science is the privileged basis and source. Whereas, for Deleuze, science provides inspiration, examples, checks and support. The stakes of this distinction can be seen in their different approaches to the relations of art and science. For the latter, art and science fit into an overall metaphysics, but with different roles. The relations of virtual to actual, and the principles and concepts that characterise them, hold for both - although with different emphases and parts to play with respect to them.

For the former, art is outside the dialectics of truth as developed and defined through science. Science is related to the past through a sense of progress, whereas art has to break with the past: 'The poetic image is not subjected to a thrust. It is not the echo of a past.'[19] This difference is a product of their opposition with respect to continuity and discontinuity. In a metaphysics privileging continuity, there is no scope for the radical distinctions of a dialectics based on discontinuity.

Given the variety of Bachelard's arguments against temporal continuity and hence against the primacy of ontological continuity, I will list them here separately:

1) Positive judgements about reality depend on negative judgements. So any affirmed plenitude depends on negations. Scientific method does not show us that the real must be approached as full and continuous, instead it emerges from a dialectics of assumptions about emptiness and fullness, truth and error (DD, 14);

2) Action presupposes the possibility of negation and hence supports the notion of discontinuity. When we make choices or assume that something functions, we do so with the possibility that we could also refuse to act or that the mechanism could fail to function (DD, 22) (DD, 74);

3) Our experience of time is necessarily a judgement of time, in the sense where we make decisions about which times to focus on and consider. Time is the subject of an inner observation that presupposes that time can be divided by judgement in order to be observed (36);

4) In terms of causality and sub-atomic observation, measurement and hence discontinuity is all-important. Physics shows reality as discontinuous passages. Time must reflect that discontinuity and duration, defined as continuous, is a false assumption (63);

5) In terms of psychology, continuity is in fact the product of a dialectical process of discontinuous moves from present to past and present to future. Continuity is an effect of discontinuity where time is cut up through processes of rejection and projection (125).

When we consider these points in relation to Deleuze's arguments in *Difference and Repetition* each point is given an explicit rejoinder. We have already seen that the remarks on judgement, will and time (2, 3, 5) are responded to through transcendental deductions of passive syntheses of time as continuous.

However it is important to remember that already in *La philosophie du non*, Bachelard developed a critique of the Kantian transcendental. According to Bachelard's dialectics, the problem with Kant's model is that there is no general object or intuition from whence to deduce a priori categories: 'Since the world of the general object is divided, the *I think* corresponding to generalisation is itself divided. The *I think* must have a dialectical activity; it must mobilise itself and be alert within a philosophy of the no.'[20] The negations and adjunctions proper to dialectics take precedence over transcendental moves and disqualify them in their claims to universality. So the key issue becomes whether Deleuze's development of transcendental philosophy avoids this kind of criticism. Given the fluidity and reciprocal relations that hold between the virtual conditions and the actual in his metaphysics, he can agree to Bachelard's critique of Kant but also answer that his own model is neither dependent on a general object, nor incapable of mobilisation at the level of the virtual.

Furthermore, on the first point listed above - on error and negation - Deleuze can answer through a critique of the fundamental role of error in philosophy and, by extension, in the sciences (DR, 150). In *Difference and Repetition*, Deleuze argues that to think of problems in terms of errors and correct solutions is to misunderstand the deeper nature of problems as irresolvable tensions between Ideas. Problems are to be repeated and transformed productively, but never fully solved. So when Bachelard says that error and negation are essential aspects of science, Deleuze need not even dispute the claim.

Deleuze's point is rather that there is a deeper condition for the scientific drive to experiment and theorise about reality. This applies to Bachelard's fourth point. Underlying the movement of error and correctness, affirmation and negation we find forms of significance and value that explain why we seek correctness and affirmation. These Ideal transcendental conditions are not tied to any given scientific theory, but they depend on continuity as one of their key premises (notably because discontinuity would be a first step towards solutions rather than productive repetitions).

How radical is the new?

Bachelard and Deleuze are concerned with the openness implied by novelty. They design forms of dialectics that subject what is known and identified to constant reformulations and transformations. However, the question 'How radical is the new?' separates the two thinkers around the form of reality implied by the new in terms of continuity and discontinuity.

For Bachelard, the new is radical to the point of implying real discontinuity that must be accommodated by a dialectics that relates things in an open and revisable manner through tensions between theories and between theories and objects of observation. Given discontinuity, thought must be of the form of a rational dialogue that holds oppositions and contradictions together through the aim of greater integration, but without a perfect resolution. He defends a difficult progress where new steps allow for a more complete and accurate relation of theory to object, but where earlier theories maintain a relative value and some resistance to incorporation into an overarching final theory.

In Deleuze's work, the new is radical in such a way as to imply a virtual continuity standing as condition for an actual identifiable discontinuity. The condition for a novelty that goes beyond all current identifications is a realm of virtual intensities and Ideas that returns in different configurations each time they are expressed in actual novelties or creations. For these creations to have the radical nature associated with the powerful sensations and significance that accompany them, the expressed intensities and Ideas cannot allow for a prior limitations on expression: they have to be continuous multiplicities of varying relations.

Notes

1) G. Deleuze, *Nietzsche and Philosophy*, Trans. H. Tomlinson (New York: Columbia, 1983) esp. chap 5, sec. 4.

2) G. Deleuze, *Différence et répétition* (Paris PUF, 1968). Trans. P. Patton *Difference and Repetition* (London: Athlone, 1994) p. 162, hereafter DR. See also J. Williams Gilles Deleuze's *Difference and Repetition: a Critical Introduction and Guide*, pp 17-21, hereafter GDDR.

3) G. Bachelard, *Dialectique de la durée* (Paris: PUF, 1950) p 150. My translations.

4) Gilles Deleuze, *The Fold: Leibniz and the Baroque* (London: Athlone, 1993) pp 134-5.

5) A. N. Whitehead, *Science and the Modern World* (Cambridge University Press, 1928)

6) A. N. Whitehead, *Process and Reality* (New York: The Free Press, 1978)

7) M. DeLanda, *Intensive Science and Virtual Philosophy* (London: Continuum, 2002)

8) See GDDR, pp 165-71.

9) G. Bachelard, *Le nouvel esprit scientifique* (Paris: PUF, 1934) p. 142, henceforth NES [all translations mine].

10) DR 131-33.

11) G. Bachelard, *La Dialectique de la durée* (Paris: PUF, 1950) henceforth DD.

12) There is an interesting parallel between Bachelard's argument against objective facts prior to theory and Dennett's arguments in, for example, "Quining Qualia" in A. Marcel and E. Bisiach, eds. *Consciousness in Modern Science* (Oxford University Press, 1988)

13) See Deleuze's study of the works of Curie in *Difference and Repetition*, DR 286).

14) This Cartesian influence can still be detected in contemporary science. For a critical discussion of Cartesian influences in contemporary cognitive science see M. Wheeler *Reconstructing the Cognitive World: the Next Step* (MIT, forthcoming) esp. Chap. 3 'Descartes' Ghost: the Haunting of Cognitive Science'.

15) See Deleuze's study of these processes in the films of Orson Welles in G. Deleuze, *Cinema 2* (Paris: Minuit, 1985) 138-51, esp. 145.

16) *The Usual Suspects*, dir. B. Singer, MGM, 1995.

17) G. Bachelard, *La philosophie du non* (Paris: PUF, 1940) p. 95-104.

18) Though not directly relevant to the main argument here, it is important to note that Bachelard's closeness to science dates his work more than Deleuze's and that Deleuze's philosophy is better positioned to explain this erosion.

19) G. Bachelard, *La poétique de l'espace* (Paris: PUF, 1957) p. 1 [my translation].

20) G. Bachelard, *La philosophie du non* (Paris: PUF, 1940) p. 106.

5

Deleuze and Whitehead:
the concept of reciprocal determination

'We therefore invoke a principle, called reciprocal determination, as the first aspect of sufficient reason.' Gilles Deleuze, 'La méthode de dramatisation', 139. [Unless specified, all translations are mine]

'Thus each world is futile except in its function of embodying the other.' A.N. Whitehead, 'Immortality', 687.

Dualism and immanence

Three related problems form the background to Deleuze's development of the concept of reciprocal determination in *Difference and Repetition*. The historical importance of these problems and the power of the concept in resolving them explains its pivotal role in Deleuze's work. Indeed, it is questionable whether Deleuze's metaphysics can stand without reciprocal determination - at least in the guises where its claims to validity are furthest from explanations in terms of 'metaphysical fictions'.[1]

Given the strong connection between Deleuze's and Whitehead's philosophies and their common background in the problems to be outlined below, this chapter asks whether a parallel idea of determination can be found in Whitehead's work.[2] It will be shown that such parallels exist through many of Whitehead's books and essays, but that there are significant and productive differences between the two positions.

The first problem concerns a possible accusation of dualism in philosophies that split reality into two realms, or, more properly in Deleuze's case, into two fields. Again, this division is an important area of interpretation for Deleuze's philosophy.[3] The fields can be seen as two sides of reality, as two separate fields that together constitute reality, or as one prior field from which the other declines or in regard to which the other turns out to be an illusion. Similar questions of interpretation can be raised with respect to most philosophies of immanence, for example, in Deleuze's own work on the status of substance, attributes and modes through Scotus, Spinoza and Nietzsche,[4] or in the long-standing question of parallelism in Spinoza's work and its different treatment in, for example, Deleuze and Curley.[5]

Despite Deleuze's claims to an ontology of immanence, the use of two concepts with respect to reality, virtual and actual, and the refusal to conflate the two, raises traditional questions with respect to dualism. These split into problems of interaction and problems of unity. How do the virtual and the actual interact? How do they maintain their distinction, if they do interact? Is not interaction the place to define a higher unity that denies the priority of the initial distinction?

These questions can be seen as raising technical objections, resolved through the many facets of reciprocal determination, though always with the risk of introducing fanciful innovations such as the infamous Cartesian pineal gland. But they can also be seen as introducing more serious metaphysical objections, that is, that Deleuze's philosophy should be re-classified as a philosophy of transcendence, hence falling prey to all his criticisms of them, for example, in his work on Nietzsche or his much later criticisms of Kant.[6] Such objections would weaken Deleuze's claims to immanence and univocity for his philosophy.

The second problem raised by the actual-virtual distinction does not directly follow from the problem of dualism, but it is related to particular criticisms of philosophies of transcendence. If the solution to interaction or to separateness over-emphasises one or other sides of the distinction, then there can be the formal objection that the distinction is a false one and that, in fact, everything collapses back onto the privileged side. For example, a possible return to a single realm could ensue, despite a prior division, with the claim that mind must be thought of as body if it is to have causal material properties. There can be a similar objection in terms of value, that is, that the privileging of one side over the other is illegitimate and establishes a false and destructive hierarchy. Criticisms of the devaluation of body as the legacy of Cartesianism, would be examples of this kind of objection. According to such objections, though two realms are defined as separate, the distinction does not hold when their respective values are compared and one of them turns out to be the main source of value, thereby conflating the two realms.

In Deleuze's case, this split can go both ways. He can be interpreted - either sympathetically or not - as depending on a strong materialism that brings him close to positions in contemporary science, thereby devaluing his work on Ideas in *Difference and Repetition*.[7] Or he can be interpreted as over-emphasising a new Ideal and virtual field at the expense of the actual, thereby leading to accusations of an anti-Platonism that merely replicates its biggest fault, instead of inverting or correcting it.[8] In terms of a return to transcendence, this privileging of one field over the other, leads to the claim that one transcends the other, in the sense of providing illegitimate means for the definition or restriction of its components. Such points can be made, for example, through the claim that scientific definitions legislate for Ideas, or that Deleuze's definition of transcendental conditions establishes them as sources for the fixing of actual events.

This fixing leads to the third problem. If Deleuze's philosophy is seen as above all dependent on an ontology of becoming (in the Nietzschean sense) or process (in the Whiteheadian sense), and if the virtual-actual distinction leads to an ontology where one or the other remains fixed, though related to the other, then becoming is subjected to being and to the return to identity, for example, in essences or predicates. Again, this can be seen as a technical problem: How can something deemed to be primarily becoming be anchored in being? But it can also be seen as an important metaphysical challenge: Is not becoming always secondary to being, given the requirement of prior identities, for difference to be thought?

In terms of this return to identity in philosophies of becoming or process philosophy, there is a key difference between the two thinkers: the side of reality that is in danger of being fixed by the other is not the same. For Deleuze, identity returns more readily in the actual. For Whitehead, it seems to be a factor in the world of Value or of eternal objects. Yet, despite these differences, both need answers to the following questions: Can they be criticised for elaborating dualist metaphysics? If not, can the key distinctions in their metaphysics be maintained? If they can be maintained, is it at the price of a return to identity and to being?

Immortality

A first response to these questions could be that Deleuze and Whitehead deny the key premises concerning a division into fields and realms and the possibility of treating them separately. The doctrine of reciprocal determination could then be put quite simply as follows. Whilst reality or the universe can be considered under two realms or fields, neither of these can be viewed as completely determined until it is taken in a relation of reciprocal determination with the other. From the point of view of complete determination, the virtual and the actual, or Fact and Value, or actual occasion and eternal object, must be seen as abstractions that provide the limits or boundaries within which reciprocal determination takes place and that contain the material taken in that determination.

There are significant problems concerned with such a definition. For example, as I shall show below, it seems at times that Deleuze views the virtual as *the* real, if only completely determined when expressed in a process of actualisation. Or, at times, it seems that Whitehead defines eternal objects independently of fact. So there is some sense according to which the fields retain an independence from the process of reciprocal determination. This is serious where that independence takes on an important metaphysical and practical role within Deleuze's and Whitehead's philosophies. This is because these roles drive a wedge between the two fields, thus allowing claims regarding dualism to return in many of their most devastating guises.

Towards the end of their careers - very close to the end in Deleuze's case - both thinkers wrote deeply beautiful and highly concentrated summary accounts of their metaphysics. With great originality, both approached questions of life and immortality implied in their earlier works, but not necessarily fully worked out until these late creations. The essays 'Immortality' and 'L'Immanence: une vie...' ('Immanence: a life...')[9] divert traditional questions of immortality, whilst insisting on the importance of value with respect to life. They also contain succinct, if difficult, restatements of the doctrines of reciprocal determination. Here are the key passages:

> Thus each "idea" has two sides; namely, it is a shape of value and a shape of fact. When we enjoy "realised value" we are experiencing the essential junction of the two worlds. But when we emphasise mere fact, or mere possibility we are making an abstraction in thought. When we enjoy fact as the realisation of specific value, or possibility as an impulse towards realisation, we are then stressing the ultimate character of the Universe. This ultimate character has two sides - one side is the mortal world of transitory fact acquiring the immortality of realised value; and the other side is the timeless world of mere possibility acquiring temporal realisation. The bridge between the two is the "Idea" with its two sides.[10]

> A life contains nothing but virtuals. It is made of virtualities, events, singularities. What we call virtual is not something lacking in reality, but something that is engaged in a process of actualisation following a plan that gives it its own reality. the immanent event is actualised in a state of things and a lived state that make it occur. The plane of immanence is itself actualised in an Object and a Subject to which it is attributed. But, however

80

hard it may be to separate them from their actualisation, the plane of immanence is virtual and the events that people it are virtualities.[11]

First, though, it is very important to insist that 'Immortality' is a distillation of Whitehead's metaphysics. He seeks to convey the power and essence of his thought, but at the risk of serious misinterpretations. I shall therefore only use the essay to begin to draw questions about his views of reciprocal determination, only then to move back through *Science and the Modern World* and *Process and Reality*.

Second, it could seem a big stretch to claim that either 'Immortality' or L'immanence: une vie...' are about immortality. They certainly aren't, if we are to understand the concept as the immortality of the soul, or of some kind of personal identity. Quite the contrary, both thinkers want to show that if there are eternal things, then they cannot be identifiable actual characteristics - this particular soul, character or mind. Rather, eternity, in the sense of a continuity free of the process of perpetual perishing (to take the somewhat doleful expression taken from Locke by Whitehead) lies in the field of Value or of virtual Ideas, where the identity associated with actual beings cannot be present.

Yet, eternity is affirmed by both essays in the way the virtual and Value bring something essential and life-affirming to actuality and Fact. So, though the parallel with traditional senses of immortality does not hold, a formal parallel is still valid. The transitory acquires value through the eternal. This is a formal claim since it is not about the character or content of what is eternal and mortal (the passage of a soul, for instance), but a claim about two forms of life where one is referred to the other in questions of value (the explanation of how something mortal participates in something immortal). But is this not to return to the problems of dualism and transcendence? Does value depend upon an asymmetry between perishing and eternity that implies that one transcends the other? It is in answer to these questions that both essays insist on the essential connection between the two fields through reciprocal determination.

Whitehead insists on a necessary relation between Fact and Value in the Idea in two ways - one positive, one negative. Positively, Fact and Value are only fully realised when they are brought together, that is, where fact is the realisation of value, for example, in the realisation of ideas in the actions (not necessarily conscious actions) associated with human personal identity. The eternal ideas bring immortality to the fact of action and the action brings realisation to the idea. Negatively, mere Fact or mere Value lack something essential, that is, they are abstractions that miss the necessity of realisation for complete Fact or Value in the Idea.

The concepts of abstraction, of the mere and of emphasis show insufficiency or lack in considering the world of Fact or the world of Value on its own. Instead, their essence lies in the reciprocal determination expressed as the introduction of immortality into mere passing flow for the world of Fact and of realisation for the world of Value. Here, abstraction, a form of bracketing, has a necessary role in the exposition, but this role does not imply that Fact and Value should be considered as separable when viewed from the point of view of a complete understanding of the Universe.[12]

Value plays a necessary role in the Universe for facts and for values, for example, from the point of view of judgements dependent on values in the world of facts. Without such judgements the world would not only be poorer, but simply misunderstood. More accurately, the poverty would be a fundamental misunderstanding and not simply a matter of making a less good choice of system. It is important to note that Whitehead's selection of judgement is particularly problematic from the point of view of the connection to Deleuze, given his extended critique of the role of judgement in thought.[13] For Whitehead, value enters the world of fact through judgments. For Deleuze, judgments about facts or about values inhibit the work of virtual and actual intensities, in the sense where value has to be experienced rather than reflected upon.

Like Whitehead, though more ambiguously, Deleuze insists on the interdependence of the two fields. The virtual is only fully realised as proper through a process of actualisation. Or, in another formulation, the virtual is incomplete without this actualisation. In return, though, the actual is incomplete without its differentiation in the virtual. So both realms require a completion that depends on a process within the other. By proper, Deleuze means that the virtual only acquires an individuality associated with singularities - singular features - through actualisation. This gives us our first sense of what it means to be determined. It is to come out of an undifferentiated multiplicity, into a differentiated, 'characterised', one. Deleuze draws a distinction between '*une vie*' (A life) and '*la vie*' (life) to underline this process and its necessity.

'A life' is the virtual. The virtual is the transcendental condition for every actual life, past, present and future. More precisely, virtual Ideas and intensities are the conditions for the creative process at work in any individual through its sensations. These relations of individuation - of sensations, intensities and Ideas - are the singularities that determine any individual: 'A life is everywhere, in all the moments traversed by this or that subject and measured by such and such objects: immanent life carrying the events and singularities that are only actualised in subjects and objects.'[14]

So 'A life' is not a particular life. This is why useful explanatory terms for determination, such as character and feature must be treated with great care; they do not depend on the indication of a given particular and identified being. Deleuze does not recognize the independence of any particular life from its virtual conditions. Instead, any such particular must be seen in the wider context of an actualisation of those conditions under certain singular conditions. All lives are singular expressions of those conditions, that is, a life given determinacy through its singularities. The notion of a particular life, thinkable under a general category or species is inimical to Deleuze's structure where all things are connected to all others - both virtual and actual.

This connection is a process of determination that goes from the virtual to the actual answered by a process that goes from the actual to the virtual. Any emerging subject or object only acquires determinacy in the actual through its singularities, themselves dependent on their transcendental conditions in the virtual. That is, an individuality that resists full identification and hence a reduction to sameness, depends on intensities - values - that can only come out of the virtual or 'A life'.

In 'L'immanence: une vie...', Deleuze tends to emphasise the process from actual to virtual, rather than the other way round. It would be a mistake, however, to conclude that the other relation is not important. Rather, there are contingent historical and political reasons in that essay for the insistence on the virtual. Deleuze is aware that this is still the most difficult and counter to 'common sense' aspect of his philosophy. The urge to identify reality with the actual and to relegate the virtual to the possible remains strong, thirty years after his groundbreaking work in *Difference and Repetition*. Moreover, value is still associated with fixed identities or even with actual things rather than with the genetic power of the virtual in its relation to creation. Nonetheless, a careful reading of 'L'Immanence: une vie...' shows that the commitment to reciprocal determination remains as strong as it was in the sixties.

This struggle with identity and its relation to common sense and to possibility explains why the encounters with Lewis and Harman in other chapters of this book are important, because they allow for a sharpening of our understanding of the radical nature of Deleuze's claims. Analytic philosophy provides troublesome critical angles for a consideration of his philosophy. It is not that this work needs to be treated in this way. It is that critical questions that will recur through Deleuze's work can be answered accurately, whilst also reflecting a critical gaze back on the premises of the analytical questions and approaches.

Following these two broad outlines, it is possible to define reciprocal determination more clearly, in particular in relation to problems of dualism. First, for both thinkers, the relation does not take the form of a legislation, in the sense bequeathed by Kant's transcendental philosophy (see the chapter on Kant, above). Neither field draws up limits for the other, whereby particular judgments or propositions could be judged to be illegitimate. Instead, the relation is a properly transforming one, along the lines of completeness or going beyond abstraction that I have described earlier. Value needs to be realised. The virtual needs to be actualised. Fact requires Value. The actual requires the virtual intensity of 'A life...'

However - and deeply problematically - it does not appear that this transforming relation can be a causal one, one open to induction, or even a symmetrical one, that is, where a process can be undone or traced back. There is a uniqueness to each transformation as singular event. This uniqueness is itself guaranteed by Deleuze's insistence on the role of virtual singularities, which we can define as relations resistant to identification or representation, yet conditional for determinacy.

An individual is determined by singular relations of reciprocal transformation of the virtual and the actual that make it incomparable to other individuals. These singularities cannot be represented without losing that property, which explains Deleuze's emphasis on the roles of expression and dramatisation in his work. We can only express individuality and the relation between virtual conditions and actual subjects and objects is one of dramatisation - we have to play, to dramatise, our difference.

So neither Deleuze nor Whitehead puts forward laws governing the relation of one field to another. They both insist on the role of the relation with respect to the completing of its two sides, but exactly how that completion takes place is often left very vague. This is quite deliberate and explicit with respect to science, in the case of Whitehead, perhaps less so, or less obviously so, in the case of Deleuze.

For Whitehead, science is associated with the world of Fact, though mathematics is associated with the world of Value. Neither can explain the process of realisation of Value into Fact. In his essay 'Mathematics and the good', twinned with 'Immortality' in *The Philosophy of Alfred North Whitehead,* Whitehead argues that mathematics teaches us about pattern, that is, about relations in the world of Value. There lies its existential importance. But this study of abstraction must be completed through 'the doom of realisation, actual or conceptual.' Philosophy has to go beyond science in responding to this relation of abstraction to individuality:

> The notion of pattern emphasises the relativity of existence, namely, how things are connected. But the things thus connected are entities in themselves. Each entity in a pattern enters into other patterns, and retains its own

individuality in this variety of existence. The crux of philosophy is to retain the balance between the individuality of existence and the relativity of existence.[15]

Deleuze insists on twin processes of actualisation (the determination of virtual Ideas in actual expressions) and differentiation (the determination of singular individuals in virtual Ideas). Any individual is therefore determined through the way its actual differences give form to a chaos of virtual Ideas; but it is also determined through the way its singular Idea and associated intensities undo its actual form by introducing singular transformations and intensities. This twinning is also a key factor for Whitehead in the balance of a process that assigns relative positions and a process that ensures that individuality remains. Both thinkers are responding to the problem of how we can have genuine individuality in a world where we also have genuine relativity. All individuals share the same world, but in a singular way. This is because existence is only complete when viewed as a reciprocal determination of singularity and identity (Deleuze) or a balance of individuality and relativity (Whitehead). The world is neither governed by full equivalences and substitutability, nor by full independence and incommensurability. Instead, neither of these options makes full sense and explains life unless it is set alongside the other.

Potential and identity

But how can Deleuze and Whitehead lay claim to a real, first-hand (that is, non-metaphorical) transformation that resists theorisation in terms of laws? What form does it take? Here we begin to see great differences between the two thinkers. In the above discussion, I have left a choice between different terms: abstraction and completion, lack and incompleteness. For Whitehead, the two 'realms' are separate because they are abstract, only to be fully realised in what he calls 'Ideas'. This full realisation is indicated in the metaphor of the bridge in the long quotation given above. The description of the two worlds involves stages which include characteristics borrowed from the other world: 'The reason is that these worlds are abstractions from the Universe; and every abstraction involves reference to the totality of existence.'[16] Reciprocal determination takes place between the two realms and not in them.

For Deleuze, on the other hand, the processes take place in the fields themselves. The virtual and the actual reciprocally determine one another and there is no third term between them, and independent of them. Neither is there any abstraction. Later, we shall see that this relation is highly complex and that it involves new concepts, such as intensity and sensation, that may invite claims about third terms or mediation anew. However, here we can stick to the definition that reality is the virtual and the actual. There are illusory and differently damaging false views in limiting reality to one or other field.

The difference between the two thinkers is summed up in opposed views regarding potential and identity (or essence). Deleuze often insists that the virtual is not the possible or the potential. It must not be thought in terms of a modal logic, where a distinction between possible and actual allows for a discrimination between fields in terms of reality (this is why the encounter with David Lewis in a later chapter here is so important). The virtual is fully part of reality and lacks nothing in comparison to the actual: 'The event, considered as non-actualised (indefinite), lacks nothing.'[17] Whitehead, on the other hand, defines the realm or world of Value in terms of the possible, a Value or Eternal object has a possible realisation and not an actual one: 'Thus, the World of Activity is grounded upon the multiplicity of finite Acts, and the World of Value is grounded upon the unity of active coordination of the various possibilities of Value.'[18]

Deleuze avoids any reference to identity with respect to the virtual. It is to be a multiplicity of variations resistant to identification and entering into determinacy only through relations characterised as distinct-obscure. This explains his resistance to the subject and to the object in 'L'immanence: une vie...': 'A transcendental field is distinguished from experience in not referring to an object, or belonging to a subject (empirical representation).'[19] Whitehead, on the other hand, defines Value or eternal objects as having a fixed, well-defined, essence. Their variation only comes in where they shift from potential to realised: 'The World which emphasises Persistence is the world of Value. Value is in its nature timeless and immortal. Its essence is not rooted in any passing circumstance. The immediacy of some mortal circumstance is only valuable because it shares in the immortality of some value.'[20]

These differences can be organised around a key question: How is creation or innovation going to be explained, without setting up some kind of transcendent benchmark that allows for the new to be related to that in which it occurs, whilst still allowing for determinacy? Deleuze and Whitehead offer different models for this (this difference between models is also the key issue in terms of the difference between Deleuze and Bachelard, but for different reasons; see the chapter on Deleuze and Bachelard, here). Deleuze sets up a structure where any event involves feedback through all parts of the structure. He then spends a lot of time explaining the exact form of this 'feedback', including how we can have the illusion of parts of the structure remaining free of the process and how feedback could not be understood in linear terms.

This makes the use of the term feedback merely metaphorical, if it is understood linearly - I impose it to help comprehension.

The question of metaphor in relation to Deleuze and Whitehead's metaphysics is an important one, since the highly specialised terms of their metaphysics are designed to respond to a wide set of problems and difficulties associated with the introduction of common sense expectations, meanings and values. Their process philosophies are trying to resist this introduction of unhelpful terms, but any use of metaphors may hinder this resistance. I have not responded adequately to these problems here, but a fruitful line of enquiry will lie in a consideration of Derrida's work on metaphor and metaphysics, for example in 'La mythologie blanche' in *Marges de la philosophie*. There is a particularly interesting connection with this book through Derrida's discussion of metaphor and metaphysics in Bachelard's philosophy. This is because the direction of Bachelard's pedagogy (science first, explanation later) is deconstructed very powerfully by Derrida.

According to him, even in Bachelard's work, analysed through examples taken from Canguilhem, it is not the case that we have the scientific concept first, then metaphor. Trope and metaphor are present in the prescientific phase of knowledge and they are at work in the emergence of any science (that can thrive or fail on the timeliness of its metaphors: the 'extended' mind today - Clark and Chalmers - the 'folded and unfolded' one - Deleuze and Leibniz - tomorrow?) This is important because Deleuze insists that dramatisation, including the selection of metaphors and use of irony and humour are necessary moment of any creation. Learning, defined as a creative movement between individuals, arrives with science and not after it. Moreover, the concept of metaphor is itself open to change and variation according to its relation to science and to metaphysics. This is crucial for Derrida, since he sees the problem of metaphors in metaphysics in terms of their invariance and in terms of the invariance they then impose on metaphysics.[21] I suspect that Deleuze avoids this invariance in the insistence that creation is prior to any metaphorical form and demands a break with any such form (through humour and irony).

This may also be true of Whitehead, where he invents new concepts and varies them through his works (to the despair of editors and scholars). In terms of this discussion of different definitions of reciprocal determination, he explains his model as a form of realisation, but dependent on two very different realms defined in terms of abstraction. These realms are, on the one hand, a realm of unchanging eternal objects and, on the other, a realm of ever-changing prehensions. Both are, to use another metaphor, toolboxes for the creative activity of realisation.

It could be argued that whether we opt for the feedback or the toolbox model matters little, since the heart of both models lies in an immanent process of reciprocal determination. According to this view, the differences between Deleuze and Whitehead would only concern the contingent illusions or abstractions necessary for the explanation of the process. But I hope to show that this view is mistaken. The illusions, fields open to feedback, and abstractions have fundamental roles to play in determining the exact form of reciprocal determination and this form defines creativity, philosophical method, critique and the event for each philosopher. Those roles also open both thinkers to questions concerning the transformations called for in our concepts of validity and truth.

Abstraction

To study the differences between the two processes of reciprocal determination further, I shall turn to two earlier texts. The first is Chapter X of Whitehead's *Science and the Modern World*, on abstraction. The second is Gilles Deleuze's presentation to the *Société française de Philosophie* 'La méthode de dramatisation' from 1967, reproduced in *L'Île déserte et autres textes*, edited by David Lapoujade. This is the first text to explain reciprocal determination and to place it at the core of Deleuze's philosophy. It prepares for much of the later work in *Difference and Repetition*.

Early on in the chapter on abstraction, Whitehead is careful to insist on the necessary connection of two realms - just as he will later in 'Immortality'. However, eternal objects can be defined in abstraction from actual occasions: 'By 'abstract' I mean that what an abstract object is in itself - that is to say its essence - is comprehensible without reference to some one particular occasion of experience.'[22] As I hope to show later, it is exactly this kind of abstraction of a singular idea that Deleuze refuses. For Whitehead, there can be a separation of the eternal object into three aspects: its particular individuality, its relation to other eternal objects and 'the general principle which expresses its ingression in particular occasions.' The first two aspects are abstracted from the last one.

The abstracted aspect of the eternal object is not only invariant, it is invariant in its ingression in an actual occasion: 'This unique contribution is identical for all such occasions in respect to the fact that the object in all modes of ingression is just its identical self.'[23] So ingression in an actual occasion is not judged as different due to any particular eternal object, but due to the different eternal objects in each ingression. In one case X, we may have ingressions of a, b, c. We know that another case Y is different, because we have a, b, d. The ingressions do not alter a as abstract, but in its relation to b, c and d. Whitehead goes on to conclude, again exactly as in 'Immortality', that eternal objects are possibilities for actualities, that is, they may be 'selected' or not - the emphasis on this term is to help a later remark on different understandings of selection in Deleuze and Whitehead.[24]

However, things become a lot more complicated through two further remarks. First, Whitehead describes this selection as 'a gradation of possibilities in respect to their realisation in that occasion.' This is particularly puzzling, since we could either suppose that all eternal objects are present in each ingression, but to different degrees (yet that would contradict the claims regarding identity made just before. This is the option closest to Deleuze's metaphysics). Or, we could suppose that some eternal objects are involved in the ingression and they themselves are graded. But this would raise the questions of how eternal objects can be separated from one another and, more seriously, of how there can be a selection of only some in any ingression, if we suppose endless connections between actual occasions.

Whitehead seems to lead to a merging of both interpretations in his next metaphysical principle: 'An eternal object, considered as an abstract entity, cannot be divorced from its reference to other eternal objects, and from its references to actuality generally; though it is disconnected from its actual modes of ingression into definite actual occasions.'[25] All eternal objects are related and have a general 'position' with respect to the possibility of any actualisation. So, though we have a necessary connection at the level of the realm of Value and that connection limits the possible ingressions together with a relation to a general actuality, each actual occasion is still a selection of some eternal objects and not others, indeed, if it were not, then the 'relational essence' would be variable as would be the limits it defined.

To clarify this apparent contradiction of independence and dependence in the abstraction of eternal objects, summed up in the statement that eternal objects have an essence separable from ingression but that they are also dependent on ingression in some way, it is helpful to return to the concept of gradation. On further reading, it is clear that gradation is not a matter of degrees or intensities, but a matter of relations between eternal objects. Free of relations, eternal objects have a grade zero. These are then simple: 'An eternal object, such as the definite shade of green, which cannot be analysed into a relationship of components, will be called "simple"'.[26]

Whitehead explains abstraction in terms of hierarchies of complexity. There is greater abstraction where there is greater complexity, that is, where an eternal object can be subdivided into relations of other eternal objects. We then have an inverted pyramid with a 'peak' at the most complex relation, subdividing to a 'base' of simple eternal objects. He implies that possibility is related to this abstraction: 'Thus, as we pass from the grade of simple eternal objects to higher and higher grades of complexity, we are indulging in higher grades of possibility.'[27] The key question then becomes: How are these definitions of abstraction and possibility related to ingression in actual occurrences?

The transition to an answer happens late in the chapter on abstraction. Whitehead begins with the statement that his discussion of the hierarchy and its conditions is locked into the realm of possibility, objects are more or less possible, but here possible has nothing to do with their probability of being actual, it is rather a way of explaining different levels of abstraction. When we say 'Green is more possible than' we merely mean 'Green is less complex than'. He makes this point with the statement that within the realm of possibility eternal objects 'are devoid of real togetherness: they remain within their "isolation."'[28]

Real togetherness is different from abstract relations in the hierarchy, it is a stronger relation that can only come from ingression, since it involves a selection within the hierarchy. For Whitehead, this selection involves an infinite set of relations, defined in terms of connectedness. Ingression highlights this set and its particular relations *against the background of the whole hierarchy of possibles*:

> There is a connected hierarchy of concepts applicable to the occasion, including concepts of all degrees of complexity. Also in the actual occasion, the individual essences of the eternal objects involved in these complex concepts achieve a synthetic synthesis, productive of the occasion as an experience for its own sake. This associated hierarchy is the shape, or pattern, or form, of the occasion in so far as the occasion is constituted of what enters into its full realisation.[29]

As Whitehead is quick to point out, this means that he is using two concepts of abstraction: as an indicator of levels in the hierarchy and as the process of abstraction of the associated hierarchy from the one of all possible relations. This leads to an interesting application. The simple eternal objects are more abstract from the occasion, because they involve fewer relations and hence a greater cut from the associated hierarchy.

So the answer to the apparent paradox with respect to the definition of the eternal object is that any eternal object has two sides, one in the 'whole' hierarchy, and one in terms of actual occasions. Each determines the occasion in different ways: one in terms of a general grading, the other in terms of synthetic relations. Why are both essential? The first is a necessary property of the nature of relations between eternal objects. The second allows the eternal object to be determined in an infinite set of possible relations. On the one hand, we have position. On the other, shape. Shape depends on position for its orientation, but position makes no sense without its associated senses or shapes. We cannot grasp position within an infinite set of relations without making certain abstractions through shaping dependent on ingression.

In the context of this book, it is interesting to draw parallels with David Lewis's work on possible worlds, in particular, in terms of differences between worlds and individuals through the presence or absence of universals and properties. Like Whitehead, Lewis draws a difference between worlds (between occasions, for Whitehead) on the basis of the selection of identifiable parts. A counterpart abstracts a given property or adds one (this also depends on abstracting the added property from a larger set). We can speak of a counterpart writing this same book, but in French, where writing in French is a property that can be added to the set of other properties - so long as we remove the ones that contradict it. This addition and subtraction of properties (and of universals) in order to distinguish between things looks very much like the processes of abstraction described by Whitehead.

We shall see below, and also in the chapter on Deleuze and Lewis, that Deleuze has metaphysical objections to this fundamental role given to abstraction. The role is a result of the emphasis on set theory and on a particular kind of logic by Whitehead and Lewis. This in turn explains Deleuze's concern with a counter 'logic of sense' as developed in his *The Logic of Sense*, published at the same time as *Difference and Repetition*. The issue here is not whether there is one or more logics and of which one is the most appropriate. Rather, it is about the place of logic in setting up core aspects of a metaphysics. Does logic come first (allied to a form of common sense that decides upon its worth)? Or do we have sensations and experiences that determine a metaphysics in relation to a series of logics that are assigned different roles and positions (for example, non-contradiction when dealing with actual differences, but not when dealing with Ideal relations)?

An intuitive way of grasping Deleuze's objection is that properties and eternal objects should be more like Deleuzian Ideas in that any new expression or combination of them changes the property, eternal object and Idea, so we never have a set to select from, but a series of varying degrees that we alter but do not select in. For Deleuze, the selection of parts is only in terms of actual and incomplete differences; it expresses an indirect selection of degrees of intensity at the level of Ideas.

The stakes are high here, since if we are dealing with relations of varying degrees (Deleuze) we lose the logical independence of eternal ideas and properties and gain a fundamental connectedness of all individuals (worlds). For Lewis, in direct opposition to Deleuze, properties are not relations: '... it is by having temporal parts that a thirsty person is thirsty.'[30] Neither do they admit of degrees: '... I have made no place for properties that admit of degree, so that things may have more or less of the same property.'[31] The same is true for eternal objects; they do not admit to degrees dependent on ingressions. Our response to these oppositions depends on whether we think that properties are a key way to truth in propositions or whether there is a deeper truth aligned with an individual's relation to its virtual conditions. Do we know something through its collection of properties and eternal objects, or through degrees of relations?

Deleuze's point has very wide ethical and political repercussions that deserve much longer treatment than can be given here. Briefly, the opposition lies in questions of the priority of continuity and discontinuity, in metaphysics, and of completeness and affirmation versus identity and negation, in ethics and politics. 'Only connect' is more important in metaphysics than anywhere else; indeed, if we fail it in metaphysics, we fail it everywhere else - despite appearances.

Dramatisation

Deleuze's short and dense essay 'Dramatisation' shares many lines of thought with Whitehead's chapter on abstraction. Most notably, both thinkers view the question of reciprocity in terms of the concept of determination. This similarity carries through to *Process and Reality*, in the categories, and to *Difference and Repetition*, in chapters IV and V that develop the ideas from 'Dramatisation'.

Whitehead's treatment of determinacy mirrors his work on abstraction. The double definition of abstraction, in terms of relations in the hierarchy of eternal objects and in terms of relations in the hierarchy but as determined by a particular realisation in an actual occurrence, is replicated in two definitions of the determinacy of the eternal object. That determinacy is defined with respect to other eternal objects: 'The determinate relatedness of the eternal object A to every other eternal object is how A is systematically and by the necessity of its nature related to every other eternal object. Such relatedness represents a possibility for realisation.'[32] However, the determinacy is also defined in terms of actual realisations.

This latter determinacy is itself two-fold. The actual occasion acquires determinacy at the same time as the eternal object: 'Thus the synthetic prehension, which is a, is the solution of the indeterminateness of A into the determinateness of a.'[33] So reciprocity is not only about relations, it is about two-fold determinacy at the level of the eternal object and at the level of the actual occasion. An actual occasion is determined by the abstraction it makes within eternal objects and by the wider relations that hold between those objects in a hierarchy. Thus occasion a is determined by its selection A, B, C, F, but also by the eternal relations that hold between A, B, C, F.

In terms of his own philosophy, this reciprocity is described by Deleuze in the following way in 'La méthode de dramatisation': 'Thus, it seems that all things have something like two impure "halves", dissimilar and unsymmetrical. Each of these halves is itself divided into two...'[34] So Whitehead's double two-fold determinacy can be found in Deleuze's metaphysics. This similarity is as exhilarating as it is surprising. Two thinkers from very different backgrounds and responding to different influences and problems come up with the same formal metaphysical structure. For Whitehead and for Deleuze, it is not only that the universe or reality is two-sided, but also that both of those sides are two-sided. But how they are so is quite different.

For Deleuze, there is only completeness where determinacy involves all four determinations. He defines important principles of reason for his work as, first, determinacy, and, second, completeness in terms of determinacy. The Idea has its own determinacy and one requiring the actual. The actual has its own determinacy and one requiring the virtual, or the Idea. This is similar to Whitehead, for example, in terms of the two determinations of eternal objects and of occasions - though Whitehead does not appeal directly to a principle of reason to justify this. But, after this meeting point, the similarities begin to break down. The divergence is teased out by two questions: What is the exact form of determinacy, in different cases? Or how do they differ? And, how is determinacy given through reciprocal relations? Or what is reciprocal determination as process?

First clues to answers can be found, in rather crude terms, through very different uses of concepts. In 'La méthode de dramatisation', Deleuze develops a strong critique of the question 'What?', claiming that other questions are much better for an approach to the Idea. This remark is then developed in *Difference and Repetition*, where a full critique is made of questions and of the search for essences and identity. This distinction is discussed here at greater length in the chapter on Deleuze and Harman. In place of questions defined in terms of fields of possible answers, Deleuze advocates problems, that is, irresolvable networks of tensions between Ideas.

Problems can be expressed in terms of actualisation, in the sense that an actualisation revivifies and transforms a problem, but never solves it, once and for all. The question 'What?' seeks essences and assumes progress towards final answers, or at least relative progress. The questions 'Who?' and 'How?' respond to local pressures and admit to local answers that change a wider frame of reference without eliminating it as a source of the pressures - to some degree this explains Deleuze's closeness to certain American pragmatists (Dewey, for example).

Whitehead, on the other hand, continues to seek determinacy through a definition of essences. This comes out most strongly in the abstraction to simple eternal objects, which are 'what they are'. It could be argued in response that Whitehead, like Deleuze, emphasises relations above essences and that what things are is relational (in terms of hierarchies that determine eternal objects). But this is not a full counter, since those relations depend on the related terms for their definition and for the deduction of the conditions that determine the nature of the relations. Hierarchies can only be set up if there is a prior definition of simple eternal objects that are then combined. So, though it is the case that the essence of complex eternal objects points strictly to the sub-relations, the definitions of complex and simple depends on the determination of essence: 'Thus the complexity of an eternal object means its analysability into a relationship of component eternal objects.'[35]

A further difference follows from this definition of analysability (this connects to the strong opposition between Deleuze and Harman on the relative priorities to be given to analysis and synthesis, and to the relative priority of continuity and discontinuity in the differences between Deleuze and Bachelard). For Deleuze, Ideas are not analysable, they must be thought of as continuous multiplicities of relations of variations. So, in *Difference and Repetition*, Ideas are given a positive and a negative definition: they are to be continuous multiplicities and, as such, they are resistant to any analysis in sub-identities. To cut an Idea, is to change it. In 'La méthode de dramatisation', this definition is sustained through a crucial discussion of the Idea in terms of clarity, distinctness and obscurity: 'We call distinct the state of a fully differentiated Idea, and clear, the state of the actualised Idea, that is, differenciated. We must break with the rule of proportionality of the clear and the distinct: the Idea in itself is not clear and distinct, but on the contrary, distinct and obscure.'[36] Ideas differ internally in terms of other Ideas through matters of degrees of relations, that is, through which regions are more distinct and which more obscure. For Whitehead, they differ in terms of components and not degrees.

Again, it is important to see what is at stake here. Whitehead can give much more determinate answers to what Ideas or eternal objects are, but this commits him to concepts of essence and analysis that Deleuze could criticise through a transcendental critique of the presuppositions of both essence and analysis. What are the conditions for the definition of simples? What are the conditions for the possibility of analysability? For the former, there would be a commitment to a contingent definition of the simple, for example, through the notion that a colour is indivisible. For the latter, there is a commitment to identity that goes counter to genesis: Ideas become and are nothing but becoming, only differentiated in terms of degrees.

In short, where it depends on abstraction, Whitehead's metaphysics still has negation at its heart - as shown in the metaphors of cutting out that I have used here. But he could retort with the following question to Deleuze: How are degrees themselves differentiated? If they can be measured or deduced in some way, then identity and cuts return. If they cannot, then there must be another, seemingly mystical or contingent approach.

It is in answering this question that we come to the greatest difference between the two thinkers. Deleuze introduces the concept of intensity in order to explain the individual determinacy of Ideas and of the actual. There isn't a direct reciprocal determination between Ideas and 'actual occurrences', instead, the two fields of the actual and the virtual depend on a process working through the sensations, intensities and singularities that determine an individual.

Deleuze defines this process through the difficult concept of indi-drama-different/ciation. What it means is that complete determination depends on the dramatisation of a relation of distinctness and obscurity in Ideas, through intensities that underlie sensations as they become part of an expression of intensity in actual identities. This explains why Deleuze uses the title 'dramatisation' for his important presentation. An individual creates itself in relation to the Ideas that it expresses through processes of reciprocal determination that run from the actual to the virtual (differenciation - where the Idea becomes determined) and from the virtual to the actual (differentiation, where the actual becomes determined through intensities and singularities). This is particularly elegant, but counter-intuitive, since the actual is not determined through identifiable differences, but through the transformation of, and resistance to, those differences as an Idea becomes expressed. In return, the virtual or the Idea is not determined through a correspondence to actual identifiable differences but through relations of distinctness and obscurity in the Idea that presuppose an actualisation but do not correspond to it.

This is why Ideas can only be dramatised and not identified. How they are dramatised is explained through the concepts of the individual, of intensity, of differentiation and of differenciation. Through the concept of intensity that operates in the virtual and in the actual varying relations take precedence in both realms; thereby forestalling any priority of individuality or separation. Whitehead's two-fold abstraction is added to, through the introduction of intensity. That addition brings greater cohesiveness to the form of reciprocal determination, because neither of the realms separates from the other as the source of an eternal identity. In that sense, the problem of transcendence studied in the chapter on Deleuze and Kant can be seen as a problem for Whitehead through the definition of eternal objects.

Stakes of a difference: Ideas and eternal objects

The stakes of the differences between Deleuze and Whitehead on reciprocal determination are summed up in the following remarks:

1) Deleuze depends upon and nurtures continuity in a way that Whitehead cannot due to his commitment to eternal objects. Perhaps this difference can be traced back to the different branches of mathematics at work in setting up the realms or fields in both thinkers;

2) Whitehead can define eternal objects as relations much more precisely than Deleuze, not in the sense of characterising specific relations, but in understanding complexity better. Deleuze has to depend on the much more vague concepts of distinctness and obscurity;

3) This dependence on distinctness and obscurity and the lack of analysability of relations, in Deleuze, makes his philosophy more dependent on an aesthetic creativity right at the heart of metaphysics, for example, in the concepts of dramatisation and expression;

4) Both thinkers see actualisation in terms of spatio-temporal realisations or actualisations. But, for Whitehead, a duality in actual occurrences is more strongly linked to duality in eternal objects. This allows for distinctions within the actual in terms of eternal objects, their number, arrangements and hierarchies. Whereas, for Deleuze, the actual is divided through identity and representation and that which resists it, intensity and sensation. This latter aspect is radically individual, in a way not allowed by Whitehead.

The differences that emerge in these remarks do not allow for heavy-handed rejections or adoptions of either philosopher and his metaphysics. Rather, they direct our interpretations of their works in terms of how we can stress different parts of their thought and how that impacts on its consistency.

So Deleuze is right to see Whitehead as an ally in the opposition to the dominance of identity and representation in philosophy: '... the list of empirico-ideal notions that we find in Whitehead, which makes *Process and Reality* one of the greatest books of modern philosophy.'[37] But equally we should ask whether this list, that includes terms such as 'determinacy' and 'realisation', is not restricted in its openness and resistance to identity through the definition of the eternal objects and the mathematical ideas that account for their distribution into relations and hierarchies.

This restriction operates through the 'Category of Explanation' xx in *Process and Reality* in a reprise of the earlier account of abstraction and realisation from *Science and the Modern World*:

> That to 'function' means to contribute determinateness to the actual entities in the nexus of some actual world. Thus the determinateness and self-identity of one entity cannot be abstracted from the community of the diverse functionings of all entities. 'Determinateness' is analysable into 'definiteness' and 'position,' where 'definiteness' is the illustration of select eternal objects, and 'position' is relative status in a nexus of actual entities.'[38]

Through this category, eternal objects and their realisation diminish the temporary and relative nature of actual entities that are only ever mobile accounts of processes such as prehension. If selection has to be among identities through their relations, then the form of the 'functionings' is determined in exactly the kind of categorical way that Deleuze criticises (straight after his approval of Whitehead's work) through a distinction between nomadic and sedentary distributions: '... the nomadic distributions carried about by the fantastical notions as opposed to the sedentary distributions of categories. The former, in effect, are not universals like the categories, nor are they the hic et nunc or now here, the diversity to which categories apply in representation.'[39] Whitehead's novel and un-Kantian use of the term category is not at fault here. Instead, the problem lies with the eternal object.

However, it is important to note the consequences of the loss of the eternal object and of the hierarchies it allows for. The eternity of the objects stands in contrast to the fleeting nature of actual occasions, thereby resolving the problem of the despair or nihilism associated with a mere perpetual perishing: 'There is the double problem: actuality with permanence, requiring fluency as its completion; and actuality with fluency, requiring permanence as its completion.'[40] For Whitehead, God requires the fluency of actual occasions to be complete and actual occasions require God's permanence.

The issue here is not whether Deleuze should have a place for God in his metaphysics - a move that would rend his whole enterprise. Rather, it is whether his idea of the virtual can provide the kind of permanence sought by Whitehead in the face of perpetual perishing. It is also whether that kind of permanence is even desirable.

A further suspicion could also provide for a fruitful enquiry. Deleuze emphasises identity and representation as ways of distinguishing the actual from the virtual - to be actualised is to be fixed in some way. Whereas the actual is more radically in flux for Whitehead. Does the illusory identity of the actual, eternally revivified through sensation and intensity, allow Deleuze to avoid the question of the nihilism of perpetual perishing?

Notes

1) For a discussion of fictional senses of metaphysics see Frédéric Gros, 'Le Foucault de Deleuze: une fiction métaphysique' in *Philosophie* 47, 1995.

2) See Isabelle Stengers, *Penser avec Whitehead: une libre et sauvage creation de concepts* (Paris: Seuil, 2002) p. 245.

3) See my 'Deleuze and the threat of demonic nihilism' in Banham and Blake (eds) *Evil Spirits: Nihilism and the Fate of Modernity* (Manchester University Press, 2000) pp 107-23, esp 112.

4) See Gilles Deleuze, *Difference and Repetition* (London: Athlone, 1994) pp 35-42.

5) See Gilles Deleuze, *Spinoza et le problème de l'expression* (Paris: Minuit, 1968) pp 99-112. Edwin Curley *Behind the Geometric Method: a Reading of Spinoza's Ethics* (Princeton University Press, 1988) pp 62-70.

6) For early and criticisms of Kant's transcendental as remaining within transcendence see Gilles Deleuze, *Nietzsche et la Philosophie* (Paris: PUF, 1962) p 106 and 'L'immanence: une vie…' in Philosophie, 47, 1995, p 4.

7) One of the strongest examples of a reading of Deleuze through science can be found in *Manuel DeLanda's Intensive Science and Virtual Philosophy* (New York: Continuum, 2002) where the virtual is stressed in terms of objectivity and epistemology against the transcendental reading I want to give here.

8) See Alain Badiou, *Deleuze: "la Clameur de l'être"* (Paris: Hachette, 1997) pp149-50.

9) Gilles Deleuze, 'Immanence: a life…' trans. N. Millett in J. Khalfa (ed.) *An Introduction to the Philosophy of Gilles Deleuze* (London: Continuum, 2003) pp 171-3

10) A.N. Whitehead 'Immortality' in *The Philosophy of Alfred North Whitehead* ed. P. Schlipp (New York: Tudor, 1941) p. 688.

11) 'L'Immanence: une vie…' p. 363.

12) For reasons of accuracy, I shall keep to Whitehead's use of capitals, to indicate whole realms as opposed to particulars - despite its rather jarring effect.

13) See Gilles Deleuze *Critique et clinique* (Paris: Minuit, 1993) pp 159-69.

14) 'L'immanence: une vie…' p 362.

15) A.N. Whitehead, 'Mathematics and the good', in *The Philosophy of Alfred North Whitehead*, p 679-80.

16) 'Immortality', p 685.

17) 'L'immanence: une vie…' p 363. See also Stengers, *Penser avec Whitehead*, p. 244.

18) 'Immortality' p. 687.

19) 'L'immanence,: une vie…' p 359.

20) 'Immortality' p. 684.

21) Jacques Derrida, 'La mythologie blanche' in *Marges de la philosophie* (Paris: Minuit, 1972) pp 317-18.

22) A. N. Whitehead, *Science and the Modern World* (Cambridge University Press, 1928) p 197.

23) *Science and the Modern World* p 198.

24) This reference to possibility and eternal objects is also stressed in Whitehead's categories in *Process and Reality* (New York: The Free Press, 1978) pp 22-3.

25) *Science and the Modern World* p 198.

26) *Science and the Modern World* p 207.

27) *Science and the Modern World* p 208.

28) *Science and the Modern World* p 209.

29) *Science and the Modern World* p 211-12

30) David Lewis, *On the Plurality of Worlds* (Oxford: Blackwell, 1986) p. 52.

31) David Lewis, *On the Plurality of Worlds* (Oxford: Blackwell, 1986) p. 52.

32) *Science and the Modern World* p 199.

33) *Science and the Modern World* p 199.

34) 'Le Méthode de dramatisation' in L'Île déserte et autres textes, ed. David Lapoujade (Paris: Minuit, 2002) pp 131-62, esp. 141 [all translations mine].

35) *Science and the Modern World,* p 207.

36) 'La méthode de dramatisation' p 140.

37) *Difference and Repetition,* p 284-5.

38) A.N. Whitehead, *Process and Reality* p 25.

39) *Difference and Repetition,* p 285.

40) *Process and Reality,* p 347.

6

Deleuze and Lewis:
the real virtual or
real possible worlds?

Secondly, the possible and the virtual are distinguished again because the former refers back to the form of identity in the concept, whilst the latter designates a pure multiplicity in the Idea that radically excludes the identical as prior condition. (*Gilles Deleuze* Difference and Repetition 273)

The worlds are many and varied. There are enough of them to afford worlds where (roughly speaking) I finish on schedule, or write on behalf of impossibilia, or I do not exist, or there are no people at all, or the physical constants do not permit life, or totally different laws govern the doings of alien particles with alien properties. There are so many other worlds, in fact, that absolutely every way a world could possibly be is a way some world is. (*David Lewis* On the Plurality of Worlds, 2)

Surface differences

For Gilles Deleuze, the virtual is real and no actual world is complete if considered in abstraction from the virtual. For David Lewis, possible worlds are real and the actual world is but one of many real possible worlds. Deleuze is critical of the concept of the possible, warning against any confusion of the possible with the virtual. Lewis's arguments can be deployed against many of the assumptions that hold for Deleuze's virtual - most notably, against the claim that the reality of the virtual is a certainty, rather than merely a useful supposition.

Given these strong oppositions, is there any productive interchange available between the two positions? Or, do they stand for ways of doing philosophy that are so far removed that they have little to offer one another? Even if they can be related, will this relation be one of rapid dismissive arguments, where one or other premise is rejected as too far-fetched (for example, that the virtual is real but inaccessible to direct knowledge or that reality can be thought of adequately in terms of properties)?

Though there is some truth in the view of a great, perhaps even insuperable distance between the two thinkers, there are important lessons to be drawn from considering them together. This is not only because they provide critical arguments that force each other into sharper distinction, but because there is much to learn about the different roles and forms to be taken by metaphysics. Lewis and Deleuze are metaphysicians, of different kinds for sure, but nonetheless closer in approach and interests than is apparent at first glance. This means that a series of fairly obvious divides between them turn out to be only surface differences that hide much more productive and important deep contrasts.

For example, much could be made of the different mathematics taken as parallels and as models by each thinker. Differential calculus runs through most of Deleuze's *Difference and Repetition*. Whereas set theory is the key reference point for Lewis. Yet, in *Difference and Repetition*, Deleuze shows an awareness of the importance of set theory, in particular, in relation to his own approach to differential calculus (he sees set theory as a modern way out of having to suppose the reality of infinitesimals - DR, 172, 222). Both thinkers are careful to distinguish the claim that mathematics is important for metaphysics from the claim that metaphysics is mathematical: 'A Leibniz, a Kant and a Plato the calculus: the many philosophical riches to be found here must not be sacrificed to modern scientific technique.' (DR 171, 221) 'Good reason; I do not say it is conclusive. Maybe the price is higher than it seems because set theory has unacceptable hidden implications - maybe the next round of set theoretical paradoxes will soon be upon us.' (OPW, 4)

An equally stark difference can be found in their apparently opposed attitudes to logic in metaphysics. In his *What is Philosophy?*, written with Félix Guattari, Deleuze sees logic as a nefarious imposter, whereas Lewis sees it as a crucial tool for shedding light on philosophical problems. But even this difference fades somewhat. *What is Philosophy?* is written against a particular kind of logic (though perhaps a kind represented by Lewis). In the earlier *The Logic of Sense*, it is clear that Deleuze thinks that structure and logical relations are important for thought, but he advocates a very different and radically unusual kind of logic. Lewis does not think that there is a final right logic for metaphysics, but that logic is subject to the needs of metaphysics.

Similarly, both philosophers owe something to Leibniz, but Deleuze refers back to him constantly - writing one of his best metaphysical works on him, *The Fold: Leibniz and the Baroque* - whereas Lewis leaves the history of philosophy relatively untouched, preferring to develop specialist discussions with his contemporaries with a relative lack of philosophical historicity. This is not a point of doctrine, though, it is a contingent matter of philosophical training and inclination - one that Lewis explicitly rejects as significant.

Finally, where Lewis works in almost constant touch with modern physics, Deleuze's main reference point, in *Difference and Repetition*, is biology. Lewis's literary, aesthetic and political references are few and strongly philosophy-centered - in the sense that literature illustrates or conforms to a philosophical problem (for example, in his discussion of truth in fiction, 'Truth in fiction', in *Philosophical Papers Volume I*, Oxford University Press, 1983, pp 261-75). Deleuze is a major writer on cinema, literature, art and politics. His influence is wide-ranging and, in some areas, inescapable: 'Today, let's say "after Deleuze", there is a clear requisition of philosophy by cinema - or of cinema by philosophy.' (Alain Badiou, 'Of Cinema as Democratic Emblem', in *Critique*, no 692-693, 2005, pp 4-13).

Deleuze allows his philosophy to combine with other subjects. He holds the view that subjects and faculties only reach their full power when they move beyond their boundaries and mix with others. There is not the same sense of range and flexibility in Lewis. Yet, here too, these differences are not fundamental to the metaphysical differences between the two; they are results thereof, not causes.

For example, in terms of the relation to modern physics and to biology, it is not the subject matter that is of importance, but rather, different ways of understanding relations to matters of fact. Lewis's interest in causality, supervenience and counterfactuals contrasts with Deleuze's preparedness to consider non-causal and non-supervenient relations both in terms of the relation between the actual and the virtual and within the actual. So, as we have seen in the chapter on Deleuze and Kant, Deleuze introduces a transcendental aspect in order to reflect on life, including biology. There is no similar role for the transcendental in Lewis's work.

When Lewis considers the possibility of non-causal relations, it is in worlds distant from our own. For Deleuze, our real world involves non-causal relations, that is, transcendental ones where the relation is one of limitation or determination (for example, in terms of false and true limits or in terms of what is or is not legitimate). The difference is not about the initially striking difference in interests, but in the philosophical methods brought to bear upon them. The most important sign of these differences lies in the difference between a philosophy of many real worlds and of many individuals in those worlds (Lewis) and a philosophy of one real world, but internally multiple through the perspectives of many individuals, where an individual coincides with that world, but only under a perspective (Deleuze) - one internally multiple world OR many spatio-temporally isolated ones?

Two pragmatisms

Instead of listing any further contrasts between Deleuze and Lewis, the key to drawing out the most far-reaching and interesting differences lies in the form and place taken by pragmatism in relation to thought for each philosopher. How we think. Where we think. Who thinks. Where we think best. The role of thinking. These fields draw out the most productive oppositions. They can be summed up as the difference between two metaphysical relations to pragmatism. Does metaphysics ground and give form to a pragmatics, or is pragmatism prior to metaphysics? Are problems defined and set by metaphysics or does a pragmatic attitude give direction and allow for decisions in terms of preferable theories?

For Deleuze, the virtual - metaphysically defined - is that which allows all problems and forms of life to connect in a way that does not depend upon prior divisions into species, kinds, properties, spatio-temporal locations, or subjects and predicates. (The exact definition of problems and its contrast with analytic approaches to philosophical questions is discussed at greater length in the next chapter on Deleuze and Harman.) In terms of Lewis's work, the main point to retain from Deleuze is the resistance to prior divisions. Deleuze's virtual has nothing to do with the everyday meaning of the term as an unreal electronically-produced copy or representation of reality. Instead, it is a realm deduced from actual events as the transcendental condition for their resistance to identity and for their capacity to become other.

So, broadly, the virtual is a transcendental realm that breaks down any given actual identity or way of identifying. By 'breaks down' we should understand 'completes and denies priority to identity'. In turn, the actual expresses the virtual and gives it determinacy. The form of the relations of reciprocal determination between the actual and the virtual gives shape to a subsequent pragmatics, where practice is an experimentation determined by the metaphysical form (that specifies content only minimally). So how we experiment is determined by series of relations defined and justified in the metaphysics. This relation between the virtual and the actual is justified and discussed in greater detail in the chapters on Kant and on Whitehead.

The status of the virtual as necessary condition for all things is a good example of this 'how', in a negative sense, where the reality of the virtual is one of the reasons why a reference in experimentation to external or transcendent (rather than transcendental) principles, values or laws is not justified. Nothing stands independent of a relation to the connecting and transformative power of the virtual; this includes values and laws (natural and moral). Deleuze owes much of this doctrine of immanence to Spinoza (see *Spinoza et le problème de l'expression*, pp 153-69).

The connection of natural laws and other forms of actual scientific explanation to the virtual is important, because it shows how any appeal to a scientific theory or explanation in Deleuze's metaphysics is contingent rather than necessary. This is even more so than in Lewis's metaphysics, because the latter takes the best science available, realizing that it is neither the last word, nor free of contradictions and paradoxes, whilst the former claims an independence of metaphysics from science in setting up metaphysical structures, but not in determining their actual content at any given time. Any theory or explanation is insufficient unless it is considered both from the point of view of individuals and in terms of its genesis and future implications - for instance, in terms of the identities and transformations it commits us to.

This means that two types of interpretation of Deleuze's philosophy are false. First, he is not committed to any given scientific theory, method or explanation for his account of the actual; instead, the actual is determined by all processes of identification and representation, rather than any given one. Second, it is a fatal mistake to define the virtual through any given scientific theory or set of theories, or even a looser set of explanations. It does not matter how 'process-like' and 'committed to difference' these theories are. They still involve identifications, limitations and negations that require a philosophical transcendental and genealogical work. We cannot take Kant, Nietzsche and Foucault out of Deleuze without losing the metaphysical openness he works so hard to achieve. If we do so, we return him to forms of dogmatism, bound to fail with the theories and explanations they wed themselves to.

In a positive sense, the form of the relation of the virtual to the actual determines experimentation as radical in terms of innovation and transformation - there is no true experimentation unless expected identities are troubled by the occurrence of new sensations defying identification. This commitment to radical novelty, and to a notion of becoming that stands prior to any notion of being, is Deleuze's Nietzschean moment. This explains the great importance of his interpretation of Nietzsche's eternal return for his definition of the virtual and his definition of time in relation to the virtual (this interpretation of Nietzsche is studied at length in the following chapter).

It is worth noting that Lewis often makes use of a more traditional view of eternal return at odds with Deleuze's view. For Lewis, eternal return is about eternally returning same worlds (in varyingly complex cycles) and about the way this kind of return causes problems for identity in the actual world in terms of indiscernible 'ersatz individuals':

> Suppose the concrete world undergoes eternal recurrence, with a Napoleon conqueror in every epoch. Consider one of these conquerors: Napoleon himself. He is isomorphic to all those ersatz individuals. So we have plenty of indiscernible possibilities for him, as we should; but instead of actualising one of them, he actualises them all! That is not right. (170-1)

For Deleuze, eternal return is about the return of conditions that sunder any identity and his preferred formula for eternal return is that only difference returns and never identity:

> *It is not the same which returns, it is not the similar which returns*; rather the Same is the returning of that which returns, - *in other words of the Different*; the similar is the returning of that which returns, - *in other words of the Dissimilar*. The repetition in the eternal return is the same, but the same insofar as it is said uniquely of difference and the different. (DR 300-1, 384)

Deleuze means that the only thing that remains the same is the return of difference. The only thing of which we can be certain is that things will be different. The contrast in choosing 'return' or 'recurrence' in explaining Nietzsche's doctrine is therefore instructive: for Lewis, it is always a question of the difficulties caused by the possibility that the same things recur; for Deleuze, there is no such difficulty, since that possibility does not arise. We do not actualise identifiable possibilities but varying differences (transcendental Ideas or variations). These virtual variations connect all actual possibilities.

This contrast between the two thinkers comes out starkly in their very different accounts of Borgès' stories. Lewis reads him selectively and with an eye to resolving supposed contradictions and paradoxes in his work. The key questions are: 'What kind of worlds does this story imply?' and 'Are they plausible?'. His answers about these worlds stress the first order 'plausible' sense of Borgès' works, avoiding their deliberate and productive contradictions, whilst emphasizing the independence of worlds in fiction and of the world of fiction: 'We tend to regard the future as a multitude of alternative possibilities, a garden of forking paths, in Borgès' phrase, whereas we regard the past as a unique, settled, immutable actuality.' ('Counterfactual Dependence and Time's Arrow' in *Philosophical Papers II*, pp 32-51, esp. 36) and - commenting on Borgès' 'Pierre Menard, Author of the Quixote': 'Different Acts of Story Telling, Different Fictions' (*Truth in Fiction*, p 265).

Deleuze's approach is to ask why Borgès' paradoxes work, in the sense of interesting and fascinating us, and what that interest and this mode of working implies for metaphysics. He does not rest with the first order, but investigates the contradictions, trying to show how, if we abandon certain false presuppositions about time and eternal return, Borgès reveals deep truths about the virtual connectedness of apparently contradictory worlds and possibilities. Against Lewis, and reading the same Borgès text much more carefully ('The Garden of Forking Paths'), Deleuze does not halt with the view that the forking paths are alternate possibilities. They must coexist in some way. Furthermore, we do not have different fictions, but the same ones connected through the ways they can be told differently. Each work is the whole cosmos and the chaos it comes out of: '... the conditions under which a book is a cosmos or the cosmos is a book appear, and through a variety of very different techniques the ultimate Joycean identity emerges, the one we find in Borgès and in Gombrowicz: chaos = cosmos.' (DR, 123, 161) In quoting 'The Garden of Forking Paths' at length, Deleuze wants to stress a passage missed out by Lewis in his separation of worlds and possibilities: 'In all fictional works, each time a man is confronted with several alternatives, he chooses one and eliminates the others; in the fiction of Ts'ui Pên, he chooses - simultaneously - all of them. *He creates*, in this way, diverse futures, diverse times which themselves also proliferate and fork.' (Borgès 'The Garden of Forking Paths', trans. D. A. Yates, in *Labyrinths* (London: Penguin, 1970) pp 44-54, esp. 51) For Deleuze and for Borgès, the creation or selection of a possibility is also a creation and selection under a particular guise of all possibilities and their conditions: '... "Every man should be capable of all ideas and I understand that in the future this will be the case."' ('Pierre Menard, Author of the Quixote' in *Labyrinths*, pp 62-71, esp. 70)

This difference in interpretation exposes the stark oppositions in methods between the two thinkers. Deleuze seems overly restrictive about possibilities and overly ambitious about difference. Why shouldn't we think in terms of the return of the same, if that's helpful and since we can? Whereas Lewis seems overly generous to possibilities. Even if we can think of such return, it seems very far-fetched and therefore unlikely. (This is a very standard criticism of Lewis in the literature. One to which he has a series of well-worked out responses based on the usefulness of such possibilities - including cases of eternal recurrence. The discussion turns on the different merits of considering possible worlds as real or as fictional, in some sense).

However, the opposition is more subtle than it first appears. Deleuze is not committed to saying that we cannot think in terms of the return of the same, but rather, that such thinking is incomplete and illusory. So the crux of his argument turns on whether he can demonstrate this incompleteness (for example through transcendental deductions of the virtual, see the chapter on Kant and Deleuze). Lewis does not claim that the actual world should be thought of in terms of eternal recurrence, but rather that this thought is helpful in defining identity in the actual world. Similarly, he is not committed to an outright denial of difference in the radical Deleuzian sense, but rather to the thought that this is not a helpful way of thinking about possibility (see the final section, here, on isolation).

For Lewis, the possible is that which allows for illuminating distinctions between parts and worlds, in order to allow for more useful reflection on philosophical problems - notably, in order to show the best applications of terms such as identity, properties and universals. In this sense, the pragmatism of usefulness is prior to metaphysics and allows us to cut between different ones, as well as serving as tool within more narrow theories, for example, in philosophies of language: 'Possible worlds and individuals are useful not only in connection with thought but also for the analysis of language.' (OPW, 40)

The contrast between connectedness in Deleuze and separation (or isolation) in Lewis is very important, because it is the most insuperable difference between them and because it contrasts two different approaches to immanence. Is immanence to be a claim about a powerful real connectedness, or a claim about the way reflection can connect across causally isolated worlds? In other words, is immanence a claim about the connectedness of all relations (Deleuze) or about the connectedness of some intellectual relations despite evidence to necessary spatio-temporal and causal independence for others (Lewis).

The role and form of thought is at stake here. Is it an irreducibly connected process - one of many (sensual, unconscious, physical, transcendental) that it cannot abstract from? Or is it a way of representing isolated worlds that affords a useful abstraction with results that are applicable in the actual worlds? Do we think best primarily through analysis and abstraction or through synthesis and experimental connections? Or should we think through both, always guided by a search for completeness, but giving priority to transforming syntheses?

These questions are strong clues for the explanation of the possible-virtual distinction. Lewis uses possible but real because possible worlds are useful (hence worth taking as real) despite their isolation from the actual world. Deleuze uses virtual because, though it is not an actual realm, the virtual is real in the full sense of a reciprocal relation to the actual one (real, but not merely as possible). This difference appeared earlier in this book in the discussions on Deleuze and Bachelard - around the difference to be drawn between metaphysics that prioritise continuity and those that prioritise discontinuity - and in the discussions of Deleuze and Whitehead - around the difference between abstraction within a set of elements and selection of degrees within a continuous series of relations.

A basic Deleuzian question to put to Lewis's position is then: 'If the idea of a possible world is useful and applicable, then is it not the case that in some way isolated worlds and reflection upon them has an effect in the actual world; therefore, is it not a mistake to say that the worlds are causally isolated?' A retort that could come back from Lewis is: 'If the virtual and the actual are connected in the extreme way put forward by Deleuze, what form of causal or quasi-causal spatio-temporal relations relate disparate things like chimera and well-understood physical causal processes?'

Lewis's *On the Plurality of Worlds*, defines possible worlds quite thinly and in a logically dense and rich way, then spends a lot of time showing their practical worth. For example, in allowing for a clear and consistent definition of counterfactuals, possible world theory and the doctrine of the reality of possible worlds provide an important tool for reflecting on theories in terms of their consistency, robustness, their relative worth and on their plausibility in applying to the actual world.

The role of counterfactuals ('If this were the case, then...') is very important in understanding the difference between Deleuze and Lewis, notably in terms of their different takes on a Humean inheritance (Humean supervenience with Lewis, Deleuze's early Hume book and its legacy for the rest of his work in terms of habit, synthesis, association and definitions of subjectivity). These contrasts and connections require a fuller work and must be kept in reserve here; for an excellent discussion of Deleuze's work on Hume see Constantin Boundas's 'Deleuze, Empiricism and the Struggle for Subjectivity" in Deleuze's Hume book, *Empiricism and Subjectivity: an Essay on Hume's Theory of Human Nature* (New York: Columbia University Press, 1991) pp 1-19.

A special definition of the difference between analytic and synthetic philosophy is a consequence of these differences between different kinds of pragmatism. Deleuze's synthesis has a metaphysical justification. His philosophy sets synthesis at its core, believing that thought proceeds primarily through synthesis, albeit with a necessary relation to analysis and identification through opposition. This is because his metaphysics defines the real as essentially synthetic and as requiring a treatment in terms of further synthe-ses, in order to be approached truthfully. Synthesis and analysis are both necessary, but neither is complete without reference to a reciprocal determi-nation of one another. Furthermore, the form of that reciprocal determination is given by synthesis, which can therefore be taken as prior.

Lewis's philosophy has analysis at its core, believing that analysis is the best way to resolve problems often traceable to muddled syntheses. Yet, this does not have the same fixed metaphysical position as Deleuze's. If better metaphysical and theoretical candidates appear, then the metaphysics should change. Furthermore, the metaphysics itself cannot be the arbiter of what is 'best': 'Maybe - and this is the doubt that most interests me - the benefits are not worth the costs, because they can be had more cheaply elsewhere.' (OPW, 5) The cost-benefits calculation is not in itself metaphysical, though this raises the crucial question of exactly what it is and how it can be defined in terms of a relative independence from metaphysics.

A possible candidate for an explanation of this decision-making proc-ess emphasizes the different pragmatisms at work. Though Lewis often goes beyond common sense and stresses its limitations, for example, in terms of the reality of possible worlds, he views his position as a dialogue with com-mon sense. No doubt this dialogue is ironic and not without self-undermining humour. Yet the sense of costs and benefits is a common one and grounded in common intuitions - even if it is to be applied to itself. Against this, Deleuze's metaphysics involves a thorough critique of common sense.

On common sense as conservatism

The following passage is a statement of Lewis's attitude to common sense in its relation to metaphysics both as something that can be overcome and as something that ultimately decides on difficult cases. It is therefore worth quoting at length. It comes at the end of Lewis's response to a form of objection, 'The incredulous stare'. The objection is not an argument, but rather an expression of common sense opposition that can be understood through this question: What is the point of such theoretical artifice flying in the face of what commonly seems sensible?

Lewis's response is to take on board the main thrust of the objection, but also to correct it and to show its limitations:

Common sense has no absolute authority in philosophy. It's not that the folk know in their blood what the highfalutin' philosophers may forget. And it's not that common sense speaks with the voice of some infallible faculty of 'intuition'. It's just that theoretical conservatism is the only sensible policy for theorists of limited powers, who are duly modest about what they accomplish after a fresh start. Part of this conservatism is reluctance to accept theories that fly in the face of common sense. But it's a matter of balance and judgement. Some common sense opinions are firmer than others, so the costs of denying common sense opinions are firmer than others. And the costs must be set against the gains... The proper test, I suggest, is a simple maxim of honesty: never put forward a philosophical theory that you yourself cannot believe in your least philosophical and most commonsensical moments. (OPW, 134-5)

The reference to costs and gains in this passage is typical of Lewis's arguments in *On the Plurality of Worlds* and elsewhere. It is not strictly utilitarian, but relies on common sense beliefs. This kind of strategy is found elsewhere in Lewis's work for example where he considers objections to utilitarianism and also where he discusses prisoners' dilemmas: 'The premise that you will be truthful (whenever it is best to instill in me true beliefs about matters you have knowledge of, as in this case) is just such a belief. It is available to me. At least common sense suggests that it would be...' ('Utilitarianism and truthfulness' in *Philosophical Papers II*, pp 340-2, esp. p 342.)

I want to stress six double-edged points that come out of Lewis's arguments:

1) His common sense is connected to actual opinions and to their relations to theory. The 'common' is laudably democratic and optimistic, not only in its refusal to write off opinion, but also in its empirical approach to that opinion (*Let's see what people think*). However, this optimism is also idealistic; it separates the common from its 'mob' and 'crowd' moments. Lewis spends little time on the way common sense can be created and fostered. Yet common sense is a sense - not only as a form of thought, but also as a physical and often thoughtless and negatively emotional reaction. Common sense views and reflections can hide deep forms of ignorance, self-interest, fear and hatred.

2) However, Lewis is careful to restrain opinion and to note its limitations. Common sense is not seen as an independent and infallible power. It can be wrong and needs the corrective of theory. This mitigates the negative point made previously, since ignorance and unreflective common senses can be overcome and ought to be. However, negatively, once again, the final authority on that decision appears to be a common sense judgement rather than a philosophical authority.

3) I say appears to be because there are two ways of interpreting Lewis's appeal to costs and benefits. One sense, that I view as wrong, is that there is a final utilitarian calculation available to us on the relative merits of theories in relation to common sense. I think this is wrong because, as a 'highfalutin' theory, the application of a utilitarian calculation merely begs the question: Who judges the new utilitarian theory? However, if I am wrong, then the thesis about the role of a certain difference in pragmatisms between Deleuze and Lewis will need to be revised in the very interesting direction of the contrast between two calculations: Deleuze's 'higher calculus' described in *Difference and Repetition* and a more utilitarian cost-benefit calculus. This worry notwithstanding, despite the positive questioning of utilitarianism in its relation to common sense, Lewis leaves judgement as relatively ill-defined, treating it independently of its deep theoretical and historical background. Can judgement be treated as a form of common sense when it has such far reaching social and philosophical roots and presuppositions? Even if judgement does not fall prey to this criticism, is there not a form of vicious circle in this appeal to a common sense judgement in deciding on matters opposing judgement to theory? Might there not be points where other things guide the judgement? This is something that Lewis allows for elsewhere through his Humean supervenience where theories supervene on facts: '[The Humean doctrine] might be better taken as a doctrine of supervenience: if two worlds match perfectly in all matters of particular fact, they match perfectly in all other ways too - in modal properties, laws, causal connections, chances, ...' ('A Subjectivists Guide to Objective Chance' in *Philosophical Papers II*, pp 83-113, esp. p 111) What, then, is the relation between common sense as fact and theories about common sense as applied in judgements about theory?

4) Again, Lewis is careful to counter some of the possible consequences of this dependence on common sense. He separates his version of judgement from forms of political conservatism. The former is qualified as theoretical conservatism, thus situating the judgement within an awareness of the dangers and weaknesses of bold theoretical innovations and their patchy historical record. But can this separation be maintained? Part of the judgement against new theories may be a wise resistance to high-risk and speculative moves, but another part lies in much more suspect reactions to innovations that challenge a social and political status quo. It may be possible to make claims for the separateness of the two conservatisms, but the basis for this separation is very hard to achieve on the democratic and empirical basis that Lewis has set himself, in particular, without referring to a meta-theory about judgement and its relation to populations and uses. Opinion is both scientifically and politically conservative.

5) A possible answer to the apparently light treatment of judgement lies in Lewis's extensive study and theory about belief in its relation to knowledge. The appeal to firmness of belief may be a way out of his problems, since it could allow for distinctions to be drawn between firm but unreflective judgements and deeper, even more firm, reflective ones. For example, there could be a cross-examination of common sense and judgement in terms of their status as knowledge and in terms of their freedom from ignorant and dangerous views and reactions, as well as political conservatism. So though democratic and empirical, Lewis's position need not be crude. However, the problem is that firmness of belief seems to be a bad candidate for the direction of this kind of cross-examination of common sense and judgement. Firstly, firmly-held views are often our most theory and cross-examination resistant ones (for example, in terms of matters of faith). It is no good to claim that these have nothing to do with common sense and judgement, since there have been and are common sense views about matters of faith and these often run counter to theory. Secondly, firmness of belief according to common sense is a very shifty quality, changing with context and unreliable over time - somewhat like the effective degrees of moral virtues (see the reference to Doris's work on empirical psychology in the following chapter). To remedy this vagueness it is important to resort to theory, but then the circle begins again. For example, how could common sense judge between the, at first sight, esoteric distinction Lewis draws between 'epistemic' and 'doxastic' necessity and possibility? (OPW, 27-50)

6) So, when Lewis recommends an inner inspection of belief in terms of common sense he is proposing a laudable restraint on the often misplaced enthusiasm of theorists and an equally laudable demand that they connect with common interests and beliefs. However, in so doing, he internalizes and gives a natural turn to a sense that is neither natural, nor truly common, nor ethical. Theorists will face the same problems in self-examination as they would in examining and gauging the common sense of others. There may be happy moments in this application, but this will be as much down to luck as good judgement.

Deleuze's critique of common and good sense takes place throughout *Difference and Repetition*, but it is concentrated in its third chapter. There, he studies an 'image of thought' and its eight main postulates. The point of this study is to show how thought declines into an image that restricts it and gives a limiting representation of it. Common sense is a key moment in this fall. The work in the chapter is not empirical, instead, it is an historical study of the way in which key philosophical concepts are reduced to simplifying and damaging postulates (for example, that the true leads to the good, or that thought is essentially representational). There is an extended discussion of this point in the following chapter on Deleuze and Harman.

Thus, against Lewis's 'let us see what common sense can do and how it works' approach, Deleuze sets common sense in an historical context. He provides its philosophical genealogy and thereby explains how it works. This contrast in approach is important, since it provides another clue as to the deep differences between the two philosophers. Deleuze views the genealogy as a full part of the functioning of something - in the sense where the things that something has excluded or drawn upon historically must be seen as part of its functioning.

Lewis studies something as it is now, understood to the best of our knowledge and through our analytical capacities - history counts as a record of our limitations (we remember that we erred, rather than considering the past in total as a form that still functions today). This recording is in fact one of the values of common sense and judgement, a corrective to theoretical boldness, not in terms of what it still owes to the past, but in terms of the broad skeptical methodological lessons of the past. In this sense, Lewis is less bold and less dialectical in relation to the history of sciences than both Bachelard and Deleuze (see chapter 3). It is important to remember that opinion has both a genetic past and a track record - neither are reasons for us to put much trust in it.

This distinction leads to two important questions that can be put from one side to the other. Deleuze might ask (in line with his work on Foucault and his debt to Foucauldian and Nietzschean genealogy): Is not any concept or process still in touch with the evolutions and selections that gave rise to it? When we think about something, should we not also, or perhaps above all, think with its past? Lewis might ask (in line with his understanding of the errors and redundancies of past theories in physics): Is not any thing to be understood in terms of the latest empirical-scientific theories about it? Is not the past something that has become erased in the present understanding, at least in terms of its mistaken or non-operative elements? Does Deleuze commit the genetic fallacy (of endorsing or rejecting a theory based on its past)? Does Lewis ignore the continuing but hard to detect work of the past in the present? (Perhaps this failure should be called the anti-genealogical fallacy...)

Deleuze's critique of common sense applies particularly well to Lewis's remarks cited above. This is because Deleuze sees common sense as strongly linked to judgement in the history of philosophy. He divides the sense into two connected judgements: a judgement about categories and about their values (Which sets or categories are relevant to this given situation? Which are the best, the highest, the most desirable?) and a judgement that assigns given things to those categories (In which set or category does this belong?) He calls the former common sense and the latter good sense.

Thus common sense is our shared sense of where judgement can apportion things and the value of those places. Whereas good sense is our capacity to take a given, perhaps complex thing, and put it in its rightful place. Both operate in Lewis's example. In judging between opinion and theory we first make a judgement, or series of judgements about the two options, for example through the distinction drawn between a theory that rightfully stretches common sense and one that does not. This is common sense and involves a series of presuppositions (for example, in not thinking that common sense and theory are completely independent, or by seeing two options, rather than a bigger range, or even a series of degrees). So there is a different and deeper type of common sense in Lewis's work; it is one that he does not envisage, but that is presupposed in the form of his most basic judgements and choices.

The second sense, good sense, operates where Lewis describes the 'honest' thinkers examining their own beliefs and assigning them to the two categories 'Can be held even when I am being commonsensical' and 'Cannot be held when I am being commonsensical'. The first sense has already operated on these, for example, in judging which is preferable (we should not work with theories that do not pass the test). The second makes possible fine-grained decisions about where things belong. In the next chapter, I shall show that this same distinction and dependence between good sense and common sense operates in Harman's defence of the value of trolley problems and their 'good' recent effect on moral and political philosophy.

So, at least according to Deleuze, Lewis is dealing with a twofold 'common sense' judgment rather than a unitary one. This is important because it returns the judgment to a wider series of metaphysical presuppositions about the form of that judgement. Judgement as common sense will not be aware of these presuppositions, yet they require a careful critique that undermines Lewis's claims about conservatism, as well as his appeal to a prior pragmatics.

Deleuze's first point about common and good sense is that they are not in fact empirical. We do not encounter common sense and good sense in life, but rather, we meet a wide range of errors and stupidities, ignorance and prejudice, self-interest and negative passions such as jealousy or greed. There is no such thing as a reliable good sense and common sense that we encounter regularly in empirical situations and that have been found consistently over long periods of time. They have to be formed. They change with education and context. Therefore, when philosophers take common sense and good sense as given for philosophy, they mean what they should be by right, rather than in fact (DR 173-4). Deleuze's roots in 17th Century rationalism reinforce this view, in particular, when we think of the opposition between reason and superstition as outlined, for example, by Spinoza (superstition and ignorance were and still are common sense forms of thought and lower forms of knowledge).

This move to right rather than fact makes the discussion of common sense transcendental rather than empirical. That is, the question is not only about actual common sense, empirically examined, but about the conditions that determine the pure forms of common sense and good sense. We have to abstract from all their alloys and deformations to reflect on their pure form, then deduce the necessary conditions for them, that is, the form that thought must take for them to be possible at all. In other words, what do the pure forms of common sense and good sense presuppose in terms of the form of thought? Without acknowledging it, Lewis has performed the transcendental move described by Deleuze. Lewis's appeal to common sense in weighing advantages is abstracted from empirical facts and elevated to a condition for rational thought.

According to Deleuze, common sense and good sense presuppose a universal faculty of recognition that is given priority over other faculties in the definition of thought. When we make judgements about categories and then assign things to them, we have to be able both to recognise the category and then recognise the thing as belonging to it. There is a process of representation - the representing of something in its essence or concept (what we mean by 'this' category, or 'this' kind of thing). This is followed by a process of comparison (when we take something new and relate it to the initial representation).

For Deleuze, if thought is subjected to recognition, then it will necessarily be conservative and orthodox. This is because that past is relayed through a representation that imposes a restrictive identity upon it (what we mean by category or kind X) and because new events are sifted by subjecting them to what is already known (Is a an X?). The genuinely new cannot be recognised. Genuine life, both past and present, goes beyond the identity afforded by representations. It is worth noting the contrast with Lewis, here, through his commitment to properties, universals and kinds - common sense accords well with these, but Deleuze's point is that it is pre-determined to, in a negative way.

Thus, where Lewis sees a wise commonsensical brake on theory, Deleuze sees the institutionalization of mistaken and deeply conservative forms of thought. This cannot be restricted to a theoretical conservatism, since the model of thought is more general and given credence by its role in theory. The appeal to a form of judgement prior to its metaphysical critique is socially and politically conservative:

> The 'I think' is the most general principle of representation - in other words, the source of these elements and of the unity of all these faculties: I conceive, I judge, I imagine and I remember, I perceive as though these were the four branches of the Cogito. On precisely these branches, difference is crucified. They form quadripartite fetters under which only that which is identical, similar, analogous or opposed can be considered different: *difference becomes an object of representation always in relation to a conceived identity, a judged analogy, an imagined opposition or a perceived similitude.* Under these four coincident figures, difference acquires a sufficient reason in the form of a *principium comparationis.* For this reason, the world of representation is characterised by its inability to conceive of difference in itself; and by the same token, its inability to conceive of repetition for itself, since the latter is grasped only by means of recognition, distribution, reproduction and resemblance insofar as they alienate the prefix RE in simple generalities of representation. (DR 138, 180 - slightly modified)

Deleuze's argument is that there is a vicious circle in philosophical positions that set down identity as a condition for thought. Once this has occurred it is not possible for thought to approach difference in the Deleuzian metaphysically open sense, since identity is presupposed as necessary for truth in all branches and aspects of thought - in decisions about the validity of questions, truthfulness of answers, admissibility of fact. This comes out very strongly in Lewis's metaphysics in terms of the questions that he seeks to solve through reflection guided by possible worlds. Each of the presuppositions highlighted by Deleuze is present in Lewis's work: conception is restricted to the concept and to properties; judgement is associated with common sense, with restricted test-cases and with pre-set logical rules; imagination is gravely restricted in terms of prior definitions of truth and consistency (through the precise definition of possible worlds); and perception is associated with exact properties rather than with new variations (that Deleuze defines as sensation). It is not enough to assume that Lewis escapes this circle by questioning properties and universals, for example, since the way he questions them is through a critical approach governed by forms of judgement that prioritise identity and parallel forms of logic that excludes the form of Ideal relations and difference that could provide a counter-position. Lewis's philosophy is geared to solving problems and avoiding paradoxes. From Deleuze's point of view, the motivations and presuppositions behind this already build in a prejudice in favour of identity, representation and recognition.

Justifying the possible and the virtual

However, might Deleuze's critique through recognition not be answered by remarking that commonsensical opinion and judgements play only a small role in Lewis's thought and that therefore any accusation of conservatism and misrepresentation of the process of thinking is at best limited? Lewis's work ranges over a long series of difficult technical problems and deep philosophical issues. The figures of judgement and common sense appear quite rarely within them. On the other hand, extensive logical and scientific knowledge are a great strength of Lewis's work, perhaps to a greater extent than Deleuze's.

Yet, this counter does not hold if we look at the role played by examples and cases based on opinion and judgement in Lewis's work. His works, though technical and difficult, are addressed to common sense opinion, not only through the style and scope of the examples - almost invariably everyday and appealing to common and 'uncontroversial' reactions and beliefs - but also directly, in the sense of being addressed to opinion as a key arbiter. In *What is Philosophy?*, Deleuze and Guattari define one of the tasks of art, philosophy and science as the struggle against opinion and its false claim to protect us from chaos. (WP 190, 202) Their argument is that the fear of chaos pushes us into defining thought and truth in relation to well-informed opinion, thereby avoiding 'wild' ideas and extreme disagreements. But opinion is a false guard against chaos, because it only creates the illusion of having done with chaos, at the expense of forms of thought that work with the creative and progressive power of chaotic ideas.

This type of appeal to opinion is a factor of Lewis's pragmatism, because his fundamental demand for usefulness is addressed to the resolution of the kind of lack of clarity that arises in everyday situations in their relation to theory. Lack of clarity is a problem of everyday thought and a threat to correctly formed opinion; it is brought on through theoretical scientific problems and philosophical ones. Strong philosophical reflection on science and philosophy, aided by logic, can resolve these problems and clarify the relation of opinion to error. (There is a longer discussion of Deleuze's critique of clarity and his defense of distinct-obscure relations as opposed to clear-distinct ones, in the next chapter.) Thus philosophy articulates between theory and the everyday, not only in terms of philosophical theory, but also in terms of the sciences. This is important in terms of Deleuze's critique of the model of recognition in thought, because it means that the recognition of problems takes sway over thought in two powerful ways.

First, the kind of cases that matter are ones that are already common currency. They are recognised to be both in need of clarification, yet also recognised as 'everyday' and accessible to opinion. The situation is therefore not the puzzle, but only a limited property of it (*here is the problem*) - unlike the Deleuzian problem with its global ramifications and lack of limits. Second, new theoretical resources, whether logical, scientific, or metaphysical are set to work on these ongoing recognised difficulties rather than fed into life and thought in a more creative and revolutionary manner. The task of metaphysics is recognised to be this kind of solution, rather than more broad and bold constructions. So the case needs to be recognised as legitimate as does the application of thought to its solution. Lewis's philosopher is a problem solver, rather than a problem creator; he is a *technical* thinker rather than a creative one.

The difference can be thought of in terms of the effect of a new discovery in the arts. Lewis's approach is like setting a new innovation (let's say the use of perspective) back into a prior way of doing things in order to improve and refine it and let it work on current theories and beliefs. The new is situated within a commitment to continuity of purpose, if not practice. This is exactly what Deleuze's pragmatism is opposed to. The role of creation is to question and transform purpose through practice and experimentation (let's say in questioning the social role of art through the creation of new art-forms such as Dada and surrealism in the early part of the Twentieth Century).

The point of Deleuze's critique of common sense is to show how philosophy prejudges the value of such creativity, if it fails to question its assumptions with respect to the dominance of the model of recognition. However, in reply, it could be said that Lewis shows how judgement and a conservative pragmatic approach are essential restraints on destructive and ill-regulated aspects of theory and creative innovations. Moreover, though there is a conservative damper on technical innovation, that innovation is far-sighted and radical - in touch with some of the most important and revolutionary ideas and discoveries in logic and mathematics. His relentless logical and mathematical debunking of 'muddle', that is, of a failure to think clearly by using unambiguous concepts and thereby raising false problems, are signs of this approach: 'Very often we do meet formulations that probably manifest confusion, and that are apt to cause it. I shall begin by separating questions. I think there are some good ones to be found, as well as the incoherent ones and the ones with uncontroversial "solutions"' (OPW, 192). For Deleuze's very different definition of 'false problems' and critique of the analysis of problems into separate questions, see the next chapter on Deleuze and Harman.

For example, when justifying the value of modal realism in terms of the content of beliefs (that it is valuable to think of the content of beliefs in terms of real possible worlds) Lewis shows how modal realism works in simple everyday cases, whilst admitting that these are simplifications and that there are more complex situations (for example in his studies of double-thinking or holding contradictory beliefs). His point is that cases of mistakes about content and double-thinking can be analysed and explained best and resolved through modal realism.

Lewis's position is pragmatic in relation to use right down to its heart, whereas Deleuze's is only minimally pragmatic in that sense and only after a prior set of metaphysical moves (where the sense of pragmatism is about creative innovation and revolutionary moves with respect to metaphysical problems such as openness). These metaphysical moves may well require a first contingent leap of faith or experience in order to get the metaphysical arguments off the ground at all. Nonetheless, given such grounds, the metaphysics will not be open to question by judgement in the way Lewis allows. On the other hand, Lewis's model fixes a mode of thought that Deleuze is opposed to, due to its incapacity to see life in its full variety and openness.

This difference in the relation of priority of pragmatism to metaphysics comes out strongly in the reasons given for *believing* in the reality of the virtual or of possible worlds. According to Lewis, possible worlds should be believed in because of their utility: 'Why believe in possible worlds? - Because the hypothesis is serviceable, and that is a reason to believe that it is true.' (OPW, 3) In other words, believing in possible worlds allows us to do more and better than not believing in them. Therefore, it is a mistake to try to restrict reality to the actual world, because we do not have final arguments as to why possible worlds are not real, nor do we have better candidates than possible worlds for resolving the problems they raise.

Despite an apparent closeness to Lewis's extension of the real, the arguments are very different with Deleuze. Why believe in the reality of the virtual? - Because the actual world is incomplete unless viewed in relation with the virtual. In other words, for Deleuze, we should believe in the reality of the virtual because the virtual is fully a 'part' of reality, or more precisely, because the actual is only an aspect of a connected reality where the notion of a 'part' is itself an incomplete and inadequate notion. When we think in abstraction of the virtual we miss key processes that give us a well-determined sense of reality:

The virtual is fully real in so far as it is virtual. Exactly what Proust said of states of resonance must be said of the virtual: 'Real without being actual, ideal without being abstract'; and symbolic without being fictional. Indeed, the virtual must be defined as strictly a part of the real object - as though the object had one part of itself in the virtual into which it plunged as though into an objective dimension. (DR 208, 269)

So the mistake lies in claims to full reality for the actual, or full determination for the virtual. The actual is only complete when considered with all the processes that lead to its genesis and evolution (its full past and future). These processes are neither possible, nor finally identified and fixed; instead, they are the stock or reserve of differences and changes in intensity that can light the actual and the Ideas associated with it in different ways. Any real thing is therefore a process within a structure (hence Deleuze's treatment of objects as analogies - 'as though' - rather than as ontologically prior elements; no identity is ontologically prior):

The reality of the virtual consists of the differential elements and relations along with the singular points that correspond to them. The reality of the virtual is structure. We must avoid giving the elements and relations which form a structure a reality which they do not have, and withdrawing from them a reality which they have. We have seen that a double process of reciprocal determination and complete determination defined that reality: far from being undetermined, the virtual is completely determined. (DR 209, 270)

Reality is connection and completeness in processes of becoming, rather than completeness as an object or as a subject, or as a possible world, or as this actual world. As soon as something is considered in abstraction from the processes it is connected to, or that make and unmake it, it is not considered in its full reality. To consider it as a self-contained thing is necessary, but it is also necessarily incomplete and demanding of efforts to move to further completion. As soon as possible worlds are defined as real but independent, an error has been made with regard to their connection in the virtual. If a possible world moves me in this actual world, if it connects with individual singularities, it is not independent or isolated, it is not even possible, but part of a wider reality of ongoing processes.

To call part of something real, is to commit the same error as calling only part of someone's life the 'real' life when other past, planned and present - perhaps secret - parts are at work in the background and within one another.

These may be latent, perhaps fading, but they are still at work and that work counters claims to full reality elsewhere. So Deleuze's appeal to Proust, above, is not contingent or a mark of mistaken reliance on literature, when science should be the true arbiter of reality. Instead, Proust helps Deleuze to learn about the signs that reveal the extension of a life through the intensity of sensations in the present. He also shows how ideas of actuality and possibility are insufficient for working through a complete real life - imagination and sensation exceed combinatorial possibilities extracted from actual identities and their sub-parts (*Are your loved ones divisible combinations of parts or whole indivisible worlds suffused with washes of emotions?*) Where Lewis is interested in counter-parts and different possible worlds for fictional characters (a Sherlock Holmes who lived closer to Waterloo station, for example, 'Truth in fiction', 268), Deleuze is interested in fictional characters whose lives encompass all worlds, but at different intensities and guided by different ideas: 'The taste possesses a power only because it envelops something = x, something that can no longer be defined as an identity...' (DR 122, 160)

Deleuze and Lewis extend reality out from the actual. The real is much more than we usually think or what common sense would recommend. When we think that the real should be limited to what we can indicate, that is, what we refer to and identify in this world, we mistakenly restrict our capacity to understand the actual. If we are prepared to ditch this erroneous commitment, then we shall have a much greater frame of reference for the temporary solution of problems.

Deleuze gives a series of transcendental deductions to deduce the reality of the virtual. They take the form; 'If we accept these events/experiences/sensations, then we must have these necessary conditions for them.' This is very distant from Lewis's position, since necessity does not come into his justification and since he is interested in the explanatory power of theories, their consistency and economy, rather than whether they are necessarily true. Indeed, we cannot know that they are necessarily true from his point of view.

So a familiar criticism of metaphysics attaches to Deleuze, but fails to gain any purchase on Lewis's philosophy. When done 'badly', metaphysics is a prejudgment of existence and of events. By setting down a fixed and eternal frame for thought, for example, in terms of an ontology that specifies what can and cannot exist, or what forms of existence are complete or not, metaphysics imposes a false limitation of what can occur. It fails to accept that things could be different, as such and in their deep structures. It also fails to accept its own falsifiable nature and fails to give adequate space to the question: 'What kind of occurrences could take place to disprove the metaphysics?'

Lewis is immune to this point, since he defines the reason to adopt a metaphysics as its usefulness. Were this to fade, or *a forteriori*, were the metaphysics to encounter facts or events that ran counter to it, then it would be happily abandoned. Lewis's commitment to 'Humean supervenience', as outlined above, captures this very successfully as does his commitment to physics as prior to philosophy as an arbiter of fact.

But things are not so straightforward. A key aspect of Deleuze's position is his criticism of metaphysical presuppositions that are present in any position, that is, any theory or activity has a set of metaphysical presuppositions. These must be subjected to critique: in particular in terms of their relation to supposedly pre-metaphysical claims and in terms of their errors or positive qualities with respect to other metaphysical positions. So there are counterclaims to Lewis's position and the opposition between the two thinkers involves critical arguments on both sides. This is why this book stresses the openness of Deleuze's metaphysics above all.

The discussion of the reality of the virtual rests on the fourth chapter of Deleuze's *Difference and Repetition*, 'Synthèse idéelle de la différence' (translated as 'Ideas and the Synthesis of Difference'). In the chapter, Deleuze explains how Ideas are virtual multiplicities, that is, multiple relations between variations that are resistant to identification. His definition of Ideas is therefore very distant from mental ideas and from concepts. They are understood better as complex relations between all raw or pure drives that can be expressed in a given situation.

A simplifying example of the relation between virtual ideas and actual situations, and of the notion of expression could be in terms of an actual political dispute. Underlying the dispute and its rational bases in claims about matters of fact and arguments combining them with one another and with wider theories, there is a network of desires. This network appears through the feelings of hurt and passion exercised in the dispute. It is because a final rational resolution is not available, or at least not in tune with all the feelings and corresponding claims, that there is a reference to a wider fields of desires.

Such desires are often defined in a very vague form, in terms of abstract energies, for example. The originality of Deleuze's position is to see this network in terms of well-determined Ideas. These are not particular ideas about actual things, but the pure form of the Idea as it can be expressed in many different actual situations. Thus 'to anger' is a variation that takes the foreground in the Idea of social revolution, it is expressed in different ways in actual revolutionary movements as anger about this or that. That expression also determines more distinct and more obscure relations between the variation of 'to anger' (not actual anger in actual persons) to, for instance, 'to resent' and 'to fear'.

The view is therefore that any given situation expresses these variations and in so doing has an effect on their virtual relations. Some relations come to the fore and become more distinct, whilst others are relegated and become more obscure. None, though, disappear completely and an Idea is always a relation of all variations but to different degrees through their relations. Deleuze's metaphysics is one of extreme connectivity. His explanation of it in terms of Ideas can be found in this passage:

> Ideas contain all the varieties of differential relations and all the distributions of singular points coexisting in diverse orders 'perplicated' in one another. When the virtual content of an idea is actualised, the varieties of relation are incarnated in distinct species while the singular points which correspond to the values of one variety are incarnated in the distinct parts characteristic of this or that species. (DR 206, 266)

Singular points are inflexions in the relations between pure variations, that is for example, where 'to anger' changes in its relation to 'to fear' (in the passage from a revolutionary movement that merely plans for revolution to one that acts). The connectivity of all Ideas, variations and singular points is rendered in the claim about all varieties - understood as degrees.

Spatio-temporal isolation and virtual connection

Through his metaphysics and transcendental philosophy, Deleuze is committed to forms of synthesis and to relations between the actual and its virtual conditions such that he is also committed to radical connectivity. There is no actual thing that is not connected to all others. There is no virtual Idea that is not connected to all other Ideas, but each to different degrees of intensity. There is also no actual thing that is not connected to all Ideas. Here, connected means involved in continuous relations of reciprocal determination. It does not mean causally determined or spatio-temporally related.

Deleuze's definition of time and of the virtual as transcendental conditions leads him to relations that do not conform to any given spatio-temporal systematisation, including causal ones. Instead, the virtual and its temporal syntheses are conditions for such actual systematisations, where condition means, though not exclusively, 'an extension beyond the measures and identifiable actual relations implied by any given system in order to explain further features of the system'. For example, this sense of condition is at work where we ask for the conditions for the evolution and passing of systems and where Deleuze deduces three related syntheses of time as conditions (where the synthesis of time does not correspond to any given system of time, as linear or circular, for example). According to these deductions any given system is related to those that it has developed out of and that it may now contradict; it is also related to those that it could develop into or be superceded by, again, including those that contradict it. This search for a complete series of conditions comes under Deleuze's version of Leibniz's principle of sufficient reason: every event and process has a sufficient series of conditions - these conditions extend beyond accounts of actual causal processes and scientific explanations.

However, does this imply that Deleuze embraces contradictions between statements about the nature of the world with no efforts to resolve them? Is his metaphysics prone to numerous *reductios*, to the point of embracing them? Is it a metaphysics that is, therefore, for all practical purposes, as good as useless since it permits all things, beyond rational arbitration and judgement? No. When thinking about spatio-temporal relations and about causality between actual things, Deleuze's philosophy adopts relative consistency and works with established laws and scientific explanations. Any dispute lies at the limits of such explanations, in particular, with respect to the Deleuzian notions of sense, event and significance. This means that Deleuze posits forms of relation that go beyond the boundaries of any given system, whilst respecting its rules, relatively, within certain boundaries. It means that he refuses any given spatio-temporal condition or commitment to causality the right to police what can and cannot stand as relations.

At the level of spatio-temporal location and causality, two actual things may stand in a fixed and well-explained relation (A caused B) with very large ramifications in terms of laws and other causal relations and subjection to laws, including logical constraints. However, according to Deleuze, this relation is incomplete unless it is situated in relation to intensities (why this particular relation is an event for an individual). This completion takes place through all virtual Ideas that are all inter-related and allow for contradictions and for breaks in spatio-temporal location and causality (a given same actual relation can be important and unimportant, can operate intensely at some level of Ideas, but at a very low, though never null degree at others). This conditioning at the level of Ideas for individuals cannot therefore allow for an external spatio-temporal order, a spatio-temporal grid for the virtual, since, no matter how open and temporary the order, there would be certain restrictions based on possibility that cannot hold for the virtual.

It is important to distinguish this virtual extension of a given actual relation from the view that any occurrence can be interpreted in many different ways. Deleuze is not advocating a form of hermeneutic openness, where we could speak of many different possible interpretations of a given occurrence. Instead, he is making the much more radical claim that the occurrence is in reality incomplete unless it is extended in relation to events that connect it to an infinite series of virtual relations (rather than merely possible ones). This incompletion is not a form of relative skepticism or suspension of full belief in a theory, in the Lewis sense of 'this is the best we have at the moment and all we know is that it may not continue to be the best'. Instead, incompletion is carefully determined in terms of transcendental conditions and relations of reciprocal determination. It has its key signs (sensations) and methods (dramatisation and creation), as well as its key events (encounters where experimentation leads to a requirement for radical innovation). There is no occurrence independent of an Ideal sense and that real Ideal sense connects the occurrence to all others, past and future and to all other Ideas (that do not even admit of the traditional sense of past and future or located 'here' or 'there').

One of the most striking examples of Deleuze's claims with regard to causality and location can be found in his discussion of destiny in *Difference and Repetition*:

> Destiny never consists in step-by-step deterministic relation between presents which succeed one another according to the order of a represented time. Rather, it implies between successive presents non-localisable actions at a distance, systems of replay, resonance and echoes, objective chances, signs, signals and roles which transcend spatial locations and temporal successions. We say of successive presents which express a destiny that they always play out the same thing, the same story, but at different levels: here more or less relaxed, there more or less contracted. (DR, 83, 112)

This passage means that, alongside the series of spatio-temporally located and causally related actual occurrences, we have a series of Ideal events that each of the occurrences is related to independently.

So spatio-temporal location and causal relations are completed by further relations that are independent of location and causality. These further relations add to what we understand a life to be. They introduce different senses of value and priority. They also imply that any act is not only to be considered in relation to the actual series but to the virtual one that holds an asymmetrical relation to it, that is, that cannot be mapped onto it (a relation between two actual occurrences does not imply a similar relation between two virtual events related to those actual occurrences). So though it could be claimed that, given causality and spatio temporal location, we have a certain fixed destiny, from Deleuze's point of view, since that actual destiny is incomplete, we have a way of changing it, in terms of its sense and significance, to the point where, a same occurrence (in terms of causality and location) can have a different sense. This is because of the presence of different actual intense sensations around the occurrence (how we feel about something actually and virtually changes it). Importantly, all different senses are related, but at different levels of intensity - hence Deleuze's remarks on relaxation and contraction.

Lewis's compatibilism is consistent with Deleuze's advocacy for both freedom and determinism in his treatment of destiny (see Lewis's 'Are We Free to Break the Laws?' in *Philosophical Papers II*, p 291). Indeed, both thinkers can be seen as accepting some kind of provisional determinism, whilst balancing it with a commitment to freedom (free acts with Lewis; freedom to replay differently in Deleuze). However, Lewis's philosophy of real possible worlds posits an isolation of possible worlds based on spatio-temporal location and (in some circumstances) on causal relations:

So we have a sufficient condition: if two things are spatio-temporally related, then they are worldmates. The converse is much more problematic. Yet that is more or less the doctrine that I propose. Putting the two halves together: things are worldmates iff they are spatio-temporally related. A world is unified, then, by the spatio-temporal interrelation of its parts. There are no spatio-temporal relations across the boundary between one world and another; but no matter how we draw a boundary within a world, there will be spatio-temporal relations across it. (OPW, 71)

It is important to draw out the full consequences of these statements, since they could be misinterpreted as being very close to Deleuze's position. When Lewis separates different worlds on the basis of spatio-temporal location and unites a single world on the same basis, he is denying inter-relations between worlds and insisting that relations within a world must be according to a same spatio-temporal grid. So it is not that different worlds interact, but not spatio-temporally; or that a same world has a spatio-temporal unity as well as other forms of unity. It is that this unity and disunity are the most plausible ways of thinking about worlds. Therefore, it is also that Deleuzian relations between different actual worlds due to different relations to the virtual are extremely implausible and in some cases logically impossible.

These claims to unity and isolation are crucial for a wide set of Lewis's views, for example, on identity, on events, on the paradoxes of time, on chance, and - perhaps less importantly, on truth in fiction and time travel. The test of spatio-temporal unity (often added to in terms of logical consistency and compatibilism - determinism and human freedom) allows Lewis to make a series of important definitions and draw far reaching consequences from them. All contradict or provide more limited views of things than Deleuze, first, because each of Lewis's positions is consistent with spatio-temporal location (for example, in terms of the position of an event as something that indicates a passage in time, or in terms of the view that time travel cannot be consistent with future actions that contradict their past causes); second, because no position can advocate relations between possible worlds, that is, for example, that a real possibility in another world is never in a transforming relation to this actual world (or any other, for that matter).

This contrast between isolation and connection is important because it sets up a far-reaching opposition between the possible and the virtual, where the former becomes a tool for thinking, for thought-experiments in terms of counterfactuals, for example, whereas the latter becomes a deeper ontological commitment. Though both the possible and the virtual are real, only the virtual extends the actual in all its aspects and through multiple forms of determination; the possible only does so through the mind - and only with a series of heavy restrictions. This re-enforces the opposition in terms of pragmatism and common sense outlined above, because, for Lewis, the identity and judgments regarding usefulness and good sense trump wild and outlandish possibilities. Though they are allowed as real possibilities, they are then tamed again as distant from the actual. Whereas, for Deleuze, the opposite is true. The apparent solidity and reliability of the actual is undermined and enriched through a series of virtual connections that cannot be tamed or discounted as lesser forms of reality (in the way the possible-actual distinction allows for). This explains Deleuze's vehement opposition to any confusion of the virtual and the possible: 'Comment est-ce que je vais sortir de ma sphère des possibles?' (Cours, Vincennes, 17/05/1983, at *webdeleuze.com*).

7

Deleuze and Harman:
distinguishing problems
from questions

There have been three good trends in moral and political philosophy over the last fifty years or so. First, there has been a trend toward rejecting special foundations, a trend that is exemplified by the widespread adoption of the method John Rawls adopts, in which particular judgments and principles are adjusted to each other in an attempt to reach 'reflective equilibrium.' Second, there have been attempts to use intuitions about particular cases in order to arrive at new and often arcane moral principles like that of double effect, as in discussions of so-called trolley problems. Third, and perhaps most important, there has been increased interaction between scientific and philosophical studies of morality, as for example in philosophical reactions to psychological accounts of moral development and evolutionary explanations of aspects of morality.
Gilbert Harman, 'Three Trends in Moral and Political Philosophy' http://www.princeton.edu/~harman/Papers/Trends.pdf

It is never enough to solve a problem with the aid of a series of simple cases playing the role of analytic elements: the conditions under which the problem acquires a maximum of comprehension and extension must be determined, conditions capable of communicating to a given case of solution the ideal continuity appropriate to it. Even in a problem which has only a single case of solution, the proposition which designates this case would acquire its sense only within a complex capable of comprehending imaginary situations and an ideal of continuity. To solve a problem is always to give rise to discontinuities on the basis of a continuity which functions as Idea.
Gilles Deleuze, Difference and Repetition 162, 211

Problems and questions

In his recent survey essay 'Three Trends in Moral and Political Philosophy' Gilbert Harman identifies three good trends in moral and political philosophy 'over the last fifty years or so'.[1] Roughly, these correspond to an antifoundationalism of a special kind, a commitment to abstract yet intuitive thought-experiments and a turn towards a science of an empirical and local type (empirical social psychology).[2]

In connecting Harman's survey with his critical but also appreciative and sympathetic work on virtue ethics, a deep-rooted difference appears between the interpretations of Deleuze's work given here and the three trends that are shared by different sides of many debates in virtue ethics and analytic moral philosophy in a larger sense. This chapter aims to chart these differences and reflect on some of their consequences in terms of critical arguments put from each position, not in order to give some final judgment, but in order to initiate a discussion and to give a preliminary situation of Deleuze's work in relation to some recent trends in analytic moral philosophy. This discussion is not primarily about moral values, laws or practices; it is about the methods used to arrive at such moral end-points.

As in the discussion of Deleuze and David Lewis, in terms of Deleuze's work and these recent trends, the first important point to note is that his work is strongly metaphysical, but not in the sense of an analytic problem-solving, object-oriented and epistemological metaphysics. Deleuze is not primarily interested in metaphysical puzzles, in what there is, or in what we can know. Instead, his metaphysics must be understood in the sense of complicated system building, where problems are redefined as vast inter-linked networks of conflicting ideal pressures and actual responses to these pressures. The extent and complexity of this system building has been shown in greatest detail here in the chapter on Deleuze and Whitehead. A problem in Deleuze's metaphysics is closer to the sense of a problem in macro-economics such as 'Should we raise interest rates now?' with its wide range of ethical, technical, social and political pressures and variables, than to a moral problem such as 'Is killing wrong?' that might allow for a definitive answer. The economic problem is practical and experimental. It rests upon a variable context such that no final formula is likely to be resistant to new developments or even adequate in light of all currently available information.

I have already considered the strong critical arguments that can be put against such complex and apparently abstract metaphysical systems in the chapter on Deleuze and Lewis, so the focus here is on particular aspects of methods, rather than on the overall validity of different approaches. However, the two cannot be fully separated since, in Deleuze's case, the particular methods depend on claims that rest on the extended and complex metaphysics. Moreover, the critical position against Harman that can be deduced from Deleuze's position also depends on the claim that philosophy cannot ignore this metaphysics and still make valid ontological claims. So this chapter should be read in conjunction with others - in particular the work on Lewis (for the opposition to utility and common sense) on Kant (for the defence of the transcendental turn in metaphysics) and on Levinas (for a description of the ethics that comes out of Deleuze's transcendental philosophy).

In order to draw out the difference between what he calls a dialectical approach and an analytic one, Deleuze defines the more traditional version of problems - as often found in analytic moral philosophy - as questions rather than problems. He uses the terms analysis and dialectics to set up the distinction, but his reference points are Aristotle and Descartes, rather than twentieth century analytic philosophy (though this philosophy is included in the tradition that goes back to Aristotle). The difference between analysis and dialectics lies in the presence of fields of possible solutions, for analytic questions, as opposed to a dynamic series of tensions and opposing pulls, in the case of dialectical problems. Dialectical problems do not call for solutions, but for creative transformations of the problem. Whereas analytic questions call for a study of their range of solutions, followed by an answer based on the best one or ones - or at least a negative answer that states that there are no valid solutions, or no best ones.

A question does not necessarily call for a final answer, but it is determined by the different identified answers that could respond to it. For example, 'Is killing wrong?' could allow for 'Yes', 'No', 'It depends on this subset of conditions', 'It is only a valid question in this situation', 'There are the following temporary answers that need to be reviewed in terms of the following empirical data'. The subset and review-conditions could be very large, even infinite, but this would still be at odds with Deleuze's definition of problems because he is opposed to at least three important aspects of the notion of possible solutions. These are the discrete nature of possibilities, the way they deny a broader background that they emerge out of, and the connectedness of all problems to one another, but at different degrees, for different individuals and events. For each of these aspects, Deleuze's objections are based on important aspects of his metaphysics of inseparable virtual and actual realms.

Clarity, distinctness, obscurity

As shown in the chapter on Deleuze's and Whitehead's metaphysics, Deleuze's philosophy depends on a distinction drawn between virtual Ideas and their actual expression. Virtual Ideas are continuous multiplicities, whereas actual expressions of Ideas must involve discontinuities. These actual expressions are incomplete without Ideas, but Ideas are also incomplete unless expressed - whilst they always exceed any given expression. This combination of continuity and discontinuity is the key to understanding Deleuze's position. It follows from his doctrine of the reciprocal determination of the actual and Ideal realms. As shown in the chapters on Deleuze and Bachelard, and Deleuze and Whitehead, continuity is metaphysically prior for Deleuze. This means that, though a continuous and a discontinuous realm condition one another, the continuous realm sets out problems, determines creation and conditions moves to the future in both realms.

There are two related ways of understanding this priority: eternal return and the definition of the future as synthesis. According to Deleuze's interpretation of Nietzschean eternal return, only difference returns and sameness and identity are always voided. This means that, when virtual Ideas are expressed in an actual situation, the identifiable entities and differences in the situation are transformed and lost, they become other through the new intensities that work within them. For example, from a Deleuzian point of view, a defeat or a betrayal and the emotions that accompany them change identifiable persons irremediably. The earlier person disappears; but the intensities of emotions can return in other people and other situations. The Ideas and intensities themselves do not change in terms of their components (the variations that determine them as multiplicities). Instead, the degrees of those variations change in relation to one another according to different intensities. Relations and variations become more distinct or more obscure, but they never disappear completely. So intensity works differently in the actual and in the virtual. For the former, it sunders identities and creates new ones. For the latter, it alters relations, but negates none of them: 'The nature of the Idea is to be distinct and obscure. In other words, the Idea is precisely real without being actual, differentiated without being diffenciated, and complete without being entire.' (DR 214, 276)

Differentiation is a matter of degrees (of relative distinctness and obscurity). Whereas differenciation is a matter of different identities (for example, in terms of presence and absence of properties or predicates). When Deleuze says that the Idea is complete, he means that it never lacks anything. Every virtual variation is in every Idea but more or less distinct, since any distinctness only appears on condition of carrying an obscure background with it. This is why the Idea is never whole or entire, because it does not have components that can all be equally present at the same time. This is because they vary in terms of distinctness and obscurity; therefore, though a given relation will always be at work in any given Idea, the degrees at which it works - its distinctness and obscurity - will not be the same and cannot all be present. But, since the relations are all there, the Idea is always complete without ever being whole.

This point is important, in terms of problems and questions, because of the difference it draws between 'clarity and distinctness' and 'distinct-obscurity':

> It is in effect with Descartes that the principle of representation as good sense or common sense appears in its highest form. We can call this the principle of the 'clear *and* distinct', or the principle of the proportionality of the clear and the distinct: an idea is all the more distinct the clearer it is, and clarity-distinctness constitutes the light which renders thought possible in the common exercise of all faculties. Given this principle, we cannot overemphasize the importance of a remark that Leibniz constantly makes in his logic of ideas: a clear idea is in itself confused; it is confused in so far as it is clear. (DR 213, 275)

Deleuze's argument is that the association of clarity and distinctness supports the definition of thought as a common and good sense that defines categories for things and then ascribes things to categories correctly. Thought is able to do so through clear and distinct representations. However, according to Deleuze, things are never clear and distinct, because distinctness depends upon the obscurity it comes out of. Clarity is therefore a source of error and illusion because it gives the impression that things can be distinct independently of that background, that is, that things are clear in themselves and that distinctness is primarily a matter of internal clarity, rather than infinite external relations.

A clear idea is confused because it fails to take account of the multiple relations that distinguish the idea, not only from other actual things, but from all the degrees of intensities and series of virtual Ideas that are expressed in, or at work in, an actual idea. So, if distinctness is associated with clarity, ideas and things are falsely abstracted from the processes of genesis and future evolutions that take individuals and ideas out of themselves and that are at work at any given time. To illustrate this, Deleuze is fond of Leibniz's example of the sound of the murmuring of the sea: 'Either we say that the apperception of the whole noise is clear but confused (not distinct) because the component little perceptions are themselves not clear but obscure; or we say that the little perceptions are themselves distinct and obscure (not clear): distinct because they grasp differential relations and singularities; obscure because they are not yet 'distinguished' not yet differenciated.' (DR 213, 275) The murmur is unclear, but this does not mean that it is undifferentiated and undetermined. It means that the interlinked aspects of the murmur depend on one another to the point where none can be separated from the others - hence the impossibility of viewing the murmur as clear by separating it into clear and distinct components.

In terms of the distinction of problems and questions this discussion of clarity, distinctness and obscurity reinforces Deleuze's view that it is a mistake to treat problems as if they were questions with fields of independent solutions, or as if we should at least try to reduce them to such fields: 'The problem is then no longer posed in terms of whole-parts (from the point of view of logical possibility) but in terms of virtual-actual (actualisation of differential relations, incarnation of singular points).' (DR 213, 275) A problem cannot be divided and decided upon according to how true or false, or how preferable, each solution is. Instead, it is matter of how the complete problem can be expressed in a new way in an actualisation (an application) that draws out and extends the power of the problem. This is not to 'make a problem even more difficult', but to accept that problems are difficult because the tensions and movements they draw together have a hold on us that cannot simply be resolved by cancelling or ignoring some of them.

For example, Harman applauds the attempt 'to uncover new moral principles through a consideration of ordinary intuitions or judgements about cases.' This is exactly the appeal to common and good sense that Deleuze is worried about. First, according to Harman, the cases are separated according to intuitions about key boundaries. Then, different weights or values are ascribed to each category: 'Almost everyone thinks that an early miscarriage is less tragic than a late miscarriage, that a late miscarriage is less tragic than a two year old, and that the death of a twenty year old is more tragic than that of a two year old or seventy year old.' (Harman, 'Three good trends') In this example from Harman, intuitions about the relative values of different slices of life provide principles that can guide our behavior in difficult 'life or death' cases.

The validity of the judgements lies partly in how many competent judges share each intuition ('almost everyone thinks'). The separation into cases and intuitive values can be translated into a more abstract and widely applicable principle or method for ascribing value and hence deciding on actual cases and on more practical guidelines and laws, for example, in decision-making about the distribution of funds through a health-care system: 'Our normal understanding of this value might be represented as a curve that has a positive value at conception or somewhat after, gradually rising to a high point in the teenage years, the leveling off, and eventually declining in middle and old age.' (Harman, 'Three Good Trends')

In trolley problems, common sense operates in the recognition of the legitimacy of the problem to stand as a moral marker for more difficult cases (*yes, this is a paradigmatic moral problem*). It also therefore stands in the recognition of the horns of the problem, for example, that it turns on the difference between choosing to kill one and allowing five to die. Good sense lies in the resolution of the problem, the ascription of greater or lesser value to different solutions. It also lies in the ascription of different values to different cases (*this is a better, more relevant, problem than that one*).

So good sense and common sense operate together. One providing the orientation for the material provided by the other. Without that orientation, the material would be useless. But without the material the orientation would be trivial or redundantly abstract: 'Good sense and common sense refer to each other, each reflects the other and constitutes one half of the orthodoxy. In view of this reciprocity and double reflection we can define common sense by the process of recognition and good sense by the process of prediction.' (DR 226)

It is important to note that Deleuze's philosophy need not be opposed to any of the practical guidelines and laws that come out of this analytical approach. His objections are on how such guidelines are arrived at and, therefore, on the validity and weight to be given to the guidelines, for example, in relation to philosophical and individual challenges. His objections are:

a) the categories are false simplifications of deeper problems;
b) those problems are problems for individuals and individual to them;
c) abstract ascription of cases to categories ignores that individuality and hides the complexity of the problem;
d) it is a devaluation and simplification of thought to identify it with the kinds of judgement given by Harman;
e) Deep thought happens when individuals develop a creative response to the problem (in expressive contact with other individuals - see the chapter on Deleuze and Levinas, above).

None of these objections mean that Deleuze cannot arrive at guidelines similar to Harman's. They mean that such guidelines are secondary to a higher form of thought. For example, in terms of the problem of the value of life, real thought may be taking place where there is an attempt to save a life, or live with a death, rather than in the representational reflection on abstract values that cannot do justice to the singular emotions and Ideas that flow through an individual attempt. This means that Deleuze's pragmatism is one that evolves out of individual difficult cases and the complete efforts to respond to them - to live with them creatively and each time in a singular fashion - rather than abstract judgements. Furthermore, each stated intuition may be a reflection of or a denial of intense pressures, and without a careful thought on that relation, the aggregation of intuitions is at best incomplete and at worst a false expression of the complex reasons behind intuitions. This matters, because those reasons serve our understanding of the robustness and changeability of those intuitions (for example, in the way they alter after events that have wide common effects and in the way that alteration can quickly fade, or sometimes become a longer-lasting change in our stated moral positions).

The challenge, then, is not to define moral and political thought in such a way as to 'solve' practical cases through abstract intuitions and common sense, but to connect actual and necessarily blunt and insufficient laws and guidelines to new responses to deep problems, to the history of such responses, to the extent of the problem (all the tensions it brings together) and to its singular intensities (the points where it resists and transforms any emergent common understanding or identification). Possible counters are that Deleuze's problems set the bar too high and that his problems lack coherence and concreteness when compared to Harman's approach. Furthermore, the emphasis on individuals leaves us with a range of difficulties concerning different points of view and disagreements. Does Deleuze's dependence on individual relations to problems lead to an extreme form of individualism? Does he leave individuals with an impossibly complex task?

Continuity and connection

Initial responses to these objections are that Deleuze's philosophy is not an individualism because problems are shared, though from different perspectives. Furthermore, problems can be defined very precisely according to different aspects of his metaphysics in order to allow for carefully-tailored practical responses, though not solutions, to problems. It is helpful to explain these definitions in contrast to the analytical definition of problems in terms of discontinuous fields of solutions.

For Deleuze, any definition of a problem in terms of a set of discrete possibilities contravenes its continuous Ideal side. It is not that there should not be a reference to a discrete solution, since he views this as necessary. Rather, it is that this necessity concerns a particular actual solution or expression of the problem as opposed to a full determination of the problem in terms of a set of discrete possibilities one of which could be selected. So a problem involves a selection of an actual solution against a background of continuous Ideal variations (these can be understood as tensions between contradictory 'pulls'). As opposed to a debate between options A, B or C, there is a selection of A with its transformation of a continuous background of multiple Ideal tensions. There is therefore a connection between Deleuze's work on problems and continuity, its resistance to the definition of questions in terms of discrete sets of possible answers and the encounter with Bachelard on continuity and discontinuity described in the earlier chapter on Bachelard and Deleuze.

The key opposition is much like the difference between pulling an individual out of a line-up and cutting a member out of a photograph of loved ones. In the first case, the selection might be said to leave the remaining suspects unchanged, but in the latter the gaping hole changes our perceptions of all the other individuals and their loving relations. In fact, though, Deleuze's argument is that any selection is like the cutting out case, the background is always altered in myriad continuous ways (for example, in degrees of love and dependency) and the line-up is never unchanged (for example in terms of degrees of relief and feelings of guilt and elation). Deleuze's model does not allow for fundamental part-whole or elements-set distinctions because any such cutting-up process misses the significance of deeper variable relations that do not allow for an external rule or algorithm that accounts for their relations. A selection or cut-out is always a radical experiment. Change one part and change the whole (or the complete picture and its associated ideas and emotions). We can define sets and their members but always at the cost of restricting a wider set of varying relations.

For example, in trying to analyse a problem defined in terms of maximising happiness in relation to social relations per unit of government expenditure, we could identify those relations as familial, friendship-based, work-based, sexual, community-based, national and international. We could allow for overlaps between these sets of relations (sisters could also be friends, and so on). We could develop a sensitive model of all the combinations of relations and spending options on sliding monetary scales. Still, according to Deleuze's definition of problems, our whole set-up would be lacking because the relations would be between identified individuals and because the relations would be prior selections among an open set of other relations that should really be thought of as variations rather than relations between elements. We would not really understand the emotional stakes of any solution without referring to that prior cut-up and all its metaphysical and emotional consequences.

This continuity at the level of Ideal and emotional intensities explains the necessity of expression and dramatisation in Deleuze's philosophy. There is a necessary aesthetic moment in any response to a problem. This is because any response must express how it transforms that intense background. To fail to do so would be to put forward a severely incomplete response; one that would fail the injunction to express and explain for others (but not too much or too explicitly: see the chapter on Deleuze and Levinas). Deleuze's constant references to art, cinema and literature are not incidental applications but necessary components of the expressive function at the heart of any complete response to problems, including philosophical ones. However, it is important to note that any definition of aesthetics and of aesthetic values must be internal to a problem and not externally applicable to all.

So, second, any transformation of an ideal background changes the relation of A to all other selections (B or C or…) through their relation to the background. This means that selections cannot be independent of one another. This is important because not only are solutions dependent upon one another - something that the definition of problems in terms of possibilities allows for. But the possibilities are themselves related in such a way as to make any identification of possibilities already a selection within a problem rather than the determination of one. For example, in terms of a prisoner's dilemma, Deleuze's objection is not that options for each prisoner are connected through the penalties and rewards, but rather that the many different social pressures, desires and ideas undergone by the prisoners are funnelled into a grid of (say) four possible outcomes - dependent on the nature of the dilemma this number could be greater and even infinite. This funnelling is already a selection from Deleuze's point of view. It is one that invalidates conclusions drawn from the narrow possibilities and the solutions of the dilemma to wider social and political questions - for example, concerning the rationality of acting for the common good.

It is important to note that Deleuze is not making the facile claim that 'things are always too complicated to allow for illuminating simplifications'. Instead, he is making the claim that problems are only properly responded to by actual responses, rather than thought-experiments, and that these responses have a special relationship to their ideal background (where ideal means emotional, as well as thoughtful). Furthermore, this does not mean that it is necessarily wrong to think in terms of thought-experiments when devising our responses to problems. Rather, it means that thought-experiments and claims about ranges of possibilities, that is, claims about the type and number of possibilities should not be taken as a fundamental aspect of the determination of problems or of their solutions. So his position is to question the role of possibilities both in terms of their claim to govern or to represent actual situations and in terms of their claim to determine ideal problems. This is done by connecting the two and by describing their relations.

Neither is Deleuze making the claim that some things (emotions, or intuitions, or beliefs) do not allow for satisfactory weighting or rationalisation in terms of practical problems. He is not saying 'Some things or relations are hermetic and too valuable to allow for correct measurement and equivalences'. It is quite the contrary. Deleuze's claim is that nothing can be validly taken out of a background of varying relations. This neither allows for a set of immeasurably and incomparably valuable things nor for different heterogeneous realms with their own rules that do not cross over. Instead, the claim is that all things are related, but the way they are related does not allow for an external ordering.

This means that, when Deleuze uses the term dialectics, he does not mean it in a Hegelian sense where a logic governs the unfolding of the dialectic and its accompanying ontology - for example, in terms of thesis, antithesis, synthesis. Through his *Nietzsche and Philosophy*, Deleuze is one of the strongest critics of Hegelian dialectics. This criticism is extended in *Difference and Repetition*. It means that, for Deleuze, dialectics is an essentially experimental method where prior relations are radically changed in an unpredictable manner by any experiment, or solution to a problem. By radically, I mean that no content or logic can be guaranteed to survive through time and that previous relations of thesis and antithesis can be transformed according to new underlying relations. Deleuze's dialectics deduces a necessary structure of interconnections - for example, of the virtual and the actual, and of continuity and discontinuity - but without specifying how those interconnections can evolve through time, including how they might be reviewed by later developments. These differences between dialectics have been observed in greater depth in the chapter on Deleuze and Bachelard, in particular in terms of the role of negation therein.

This necessary interconnection of problems means that any problem is always connected to *all* others and to *all* actual expressions or transformations of them (it is inaccurate to keep to the terms such as solution or resolution here, since they maintain a sense of closing a problem that is inconsistent with Deleuze's position). These connections may be very distant and faint, but they cannot in principle be discounted and they may, in fact, turn out to be important in future. In terms of the example about social relations and friendship given above, no relation is strictly irrelevant and happiness may quite well be refocused onto domestic animals, a landscape, an historical figure or an object. The reason that this can happen is that Ideal relations are not bound by things we can identify, but the multiple varying relations of degrees allowed by the feelings or sensations that accompany those things. It is not what makes you happy, it is about the infinitely variable series of different intensities that accompany any given happiness relation ('A happy with B' is short-hand for a much more complex set of varying degrees of sensations, thoughts and emotions).

This means that any given transformation through an actual situation depends on individual selections that determine degrees of relations of closeness and distance in terms of the background that things are selected out of. The selection is individual and contingent, not in the sense of an individual person, but in the sense of an individual situation among many, where individual is determined by the way the degrees of closeness and distance are expressed through sensations in the situation. So any selection of the key relations for happiness and of the things they relate is only one actual expression of an infinite set of other latent relations. These cannot be thought of as possible, since they are all interlinked and since the selection is of degrees through an actual situation, rather than of identifiable options or possibilities.

The accusation of individualism against Deleuze is therefore invalid, since he is not advocating a philosophy of solipsistic isolated individuals. Quite the contrary: his philosophy connects all individuals, but with a connection that resists external norms and values. All individuals are connected, but how they are connected is individual to each. Yet this 'how' informs all the other connections and the nature of reality. The following crucial summary passage from *Difference and Repetition* captures this connection and its relation to Ideas and problems:

> Every body, every thing, thinks and is a thought to the extent that, reduced to its intensive reasons, it expresses an Idea the actualisation of which it determines. However, the thinker himself makes his individual differences from all manner of things: it is in this sense that he is charged with the stones and the diamonds, the plants "and even the animals". The thinker, undoubtedly the thinker of eternal return, is the individual, the individual universal. It is he who makes use of all the power of the clear and the confused, of the clear-confused, in order to think the Idea in all its power as the distinct-obscure. What is more, the multiple, mobile and communicating character of individuality, its implicated character, must be constantly recalled. (DR 254, 327)[3]

This philosophy changes the focus of moral debate away from individual human minds and to the interconnection of all things as expressive of Ideas.

Moreover, as expressive of Ideas that run through all other individuals, each thinker is infused with the energy of all other things and responsible for them - in both senses of 'charged'. As connected in this way, the Deleuzian thinker must take the power of determinacy (the way it stresses and lays value on identities) and extend that value, its sensations and intensities, to the obscure background that determinacy cuts it off from. But this expressivity and power must be traced back to motion, for example, in the intense sensations that set an individual into a process of becoming that exceeds what was known about it and what it knew of itself.

In practice, this means that, in addition to thinking about practical principles and shared values, Deleuze asks us to pay attention to new events and to new developments insofar as they connect us to eternal problems in new ways. This attention is a matter of creativity - the creation of new concepts and new sensations, for example. We should always be testing boundaries, rather than trying to establish them. We should always be testing principles, rather making claims to unbreakable laws. But this kind of test must take account of connected charges and transformations, rather than categories. It must seek to create new events - to become an event for other individuals - rather than take events and distil them into more simple, clear and fixed conclusions and definitions.

So, according to Deleuze, problems are ill-defined: a. if they are determined according to ranges of possibilities; b. if the solutions to problems are not considered to transform the original problem and its relation to other solutions; c. if the problem is limited in principle in terms of its relations to other problems and pressures. A problem is therefore immanent to the acts and situations that respond to it. It is not an external view-point or analytical tool but a set of ideal pressures that drive, direct and thwart our acts; just as our acts transform the problem.

A counter to this position is that Deleuze's arguments depend on definitions of the virtual side of problems that fail to add anything to the methods and information required to solve them. In that sense, Deleuze's metaphysics would be redundant because it has no practical effect on how we approach problems. It is all very well to say that there are always more connections, more subdivisions and ongoing transformations of problems, but if that cannot be translated into practice, then it is useless. This sense of usefulness is important, not only because it refers back to the same point about use made by Lewis in terms of the justification of the reality of possible worlds, but because a similar sense of use and advance underpins Harman's judgments about the three trends: 'If philosophy is concerned to improve moral and political thinking, it is relevant if the whole notion of character is misconceived.' Harman spends very little time defining the 'goodness' in the trends, but implicitly his argument draws a connection between advances in understanding and practical moral and political benefits (to improve through understanding, itself defined as better explanation).

An initial answer to this objection lies in Deleuze's definition of the problem as both immanent and transcendent. This is not a paradox. Rather, he means that, in terms of its internal relations, the problem is independent from its cases of solution. It always exceeds any given solution (for example in terms of its extension and the degrees of relations that can be taken). There is no direct causal link between the whole problem and any given solution. However, in terms of the necessity of particular determinations of those relations and of actual solutions the problem is immanent: 'The problem is at once transcendent and immanent in relation to its solutions. Transcendent, because it consists in a system of ideal liaisons or differential relations between generic elements. Immanent, because these liaisons or relations are incarnated in the actual relations which do not resemble them and are defined by the field of solutions.' (DR 163, 212)

Truth and problems

Deleuze is consistently critical of philosophies that 'mistake' questions for problems or that select restricted or overly simple problems. This criticism is made with Félix Guattari in *What is Philosophy?* But I prefer its (slightly) less polemical form in the third chapter of *Difference and Repetition*:

> We are led to believe that the activity of thinking, along with truth and falsehood in relation to that activity, begins only with the search for solutions, that both of these concern only solutions. This belief probably has the same origin as the other postulates of the dogmatic image: puerile examples taken out of context and erected into models. According to this infantile prejudice, the master sets a problem, our task is to solve it, and the result is accredited true or false by a powerful authority. (DR 158, 205)

The objection to the tactics of cutting away from context and of setting up representative models have already been treated at length here. The point about puerility is not meant to be an insult, but a remark on the relation between the intuitive power of the question-answer model and modes of education and learning. The point rejoins Deleuze's creative pedagogy that asks for variation rather than reproduction in the teacher-pupil relation. This variation should be there right from the start and not something that comes in after a propaedeutic grounding in requisite knowledge and rule-following. Philosophical methods and their hold on our expectations and intuitions have a genealogy in methods of education.

Through these genealogies, learning becomes a matter of truth. In the question-answer model, truth is associated with the successful answer to a question and not with the drawing up of the problem in the first place. Whereas, in the learning as experimental variation model, the capacity to learn becomes a goal in itself, independent of method and knowledge. As such, truth becomes a factor of the power of learning in relation to the broad background of difficulties and productive connections that surround it. The above passage therefore adds the claim that truth and falsity are a matter of problems, rather than solutions. This is important because it extends points about the necessity of taking account of backgrounds and of individuals into a transfer from truthful answers to well-posed problems: 'A solution always has the truth it deserves according to the problem to which it is a response, and the problem always has the solution it deserves in proportion to its own truth or falsity - in other words, in proportion to its sense .' (DR 159, 206)

Here 'sense' is not the meaning of a proposition, but a complex relation of a transforming actual sensation and its Ideal background. The sense of an event is not our understanding of it, but its effect upon us and the Ideal pressures that this effect brings to bear on us. For example, we can understand that something has happened (a birth, a death, an emotional encounter) but this understanding is in no way a sufficient account of the lasting impression of the event. An ending (*It has gone forever*) may transform a life in powerful and dramatic ways, that were at work before the ending, but not realised until it happened. Once released and allowed to flow through us, in our emotions and their capacity to evade understanding, events and the tensions and drives behind them give sense to a life, not in terms of an understood meaning, but in the sense of a direction and a dynamism that we have to live with.

In the proper Deleuzian sense, problems do not allow for solutions or even ranges of solutions. But that is not the issue with respect to truth. It could have been thought that the question 'Is killing wrong?' only defines a false problem when it is answered badly, that is, when it is given a final answer that is meant to leave the question answered once and for all - and to provide us with a rule or law to use in all future cases. It is arguable that this kind of answer is very much in the minority in philosophy today (though it is equally

143

arguable that in society at large there is a renewed tendency to seek and to hold to such simplifications). But Deleuze is not only opposed to final answers, he is opposed to questions that *invite* ranges of possible solutions. Truth and falsity are a matter or true and false problems - distinguished through the way they foster the illusion of the possibility of ranges of answers.

This is because the posing of the problem is the key philosophical issue, rather than the type of answer. So it is not important whether answers are temporary, or held in suspense, or organised according to degrees of probability, or set out according to a series of counterfactuals. Each of these options still supposes that the problem can be subdivided into a set of discrete responses. This fuses the problem with its answers and loses the way the problem is meant to capture the series of emotional and ideal tensions and pulls at work in any answer. Drawing a problem well, in a way close to Deleuze's use of the term diagram in his *Logic of Sensation* and *Foucault*, means drawing the forces at work in all answers but to different degrees. Any representation in terms of ranges of answers hides both the connection that this background draws between apparently disparate answers and the source of destabilising significance it provides to each answer. The destabilisation comes from the connection to other answers through the problem and from the expression of the different tensions and pulls within any given answer.

Truth is therefore never simply a matter of correspondence or coherence, but a matter of connection and intensity. A problem is more true the further it connects with other problems, but it must not lose the intensity that accompanies narrow takes on problems, where a few intense sensations and ideas come to the fore at the cost of all others. So a problem could never be posed in a simple clear form, since it needs both to express the singular intensity that works within it and its near but also far-flung influences. Truth, then, is matter of selecting how a problem is to be expressed, how it is to work through us and through others. We never start cold with respect to such truths, they grip us through a set of imperatives - the first sense of the problem. We can then respond through actual selections in order to be true to the intensities that work through us and to their connection to all other Ideas. There are no solutions, only throws of the dice:

> The throw of the dice carries out the calculation of problems, the determination of differential elements or the distribution of singular points which constitute a structure. The circular relation between imperatives and the problems which follow from them is formed in this manner. Resonance constitutes the truth of a problem as such, in which the imperative is tested, even though the problem itself is born of the imperative. (DR 198)

It is essential, though, not to confuse this insistence on experimentation and selection with an irresponsible nonsensical 'anything goes'. What Deleuze means by calculation includes all the things that Harman would take account of, including current legislation, science, other views, stated arguments, inconsistencies and so on. But, in addition to these, we have to trace what makes these singular for us. Not where we stand, but how we are moved by new events and how we should respond to that motion. This response is necessarily creative, but not necessarily *violently* destructive; on the contrary, such destructiveness and extreme moral positions (any absolutes) are inimical to Deleuze's concern to connect to the full extent of a problem. He is much closer to a careful liberal position in morality than to any religious extremism based on transcendent values.

A new kind of foundation:
metaphysics as experimentation

In Deleuze's metaphysics, everyday objects are supplemented by strange and often counter-intuitive metaphysical entities. Indeed, this can be said of anything approached in 'real world' ostensible form or even through scientific deduction. All things have a metaphysical aspect that takes them beyond the boundaries of observation, common sense and current scientific theory.

To understand Deleuze's philosophical commitments, it is better to turn to comprehensive readings of Kant, where the three critiques and the later political essays are read together and seen as interdependent.[4] Or we could turn to Bergson, to Nietzsche, or to Spinoza in their more metaphysical moments (*élan vital*, will to power, substance).

At the very least, it is clear that Deleuze's philosophy begins quite a long way away from the roots of Harman's good trend away from metaphysical foundationalism. This trend is explained in terms of a distinction drawn between beliefs that are viewed as foundational and those that are not. Harman welcomes moves away from the distinction and toward a single plane of beliefs. Whereas Deleuze's metaphysics depends on distinctions of that type. For example, a belief in a transcendental field can be ascribed to Deleuze. He gives it priority over more prosaic ones.

So, in opposition to the move away from foundational beliefs as read by Harman, we find Deleuze's transcendental philosophy, where virtual conditions are deduced for actual events, where the virtual and actual fields are seen as related through processes of reciprocal determination, and where the structures that follow from those deductions take on the role of something like foundational beliefs. The language of beliefs is somewhat forced in this context, since Deleuze is more interested in processes. Perhaps it would be best to say that foundationalism remains in the sense that processes are privileged over identities.

This departure carries through to the second trend described by Harman. In opposition to the commitment to abstract thought-experiments (trolley problems) Deleuze studies complex art-works, works of philosophy and literary figures (for example, the paintings of Francis Bacon, the works of Spinoza and Leibniz, Proust's *In Search of Lost Time*).

However, Deleuze retains the vocabulary of experimentation and empiricism, but in a very different sense. Experimentation is the individual transformation of a complex metaphysical situation, where focusing on an abstract problem would be an error due to false abstractness. A particularly explicit first attack on this false abstraction, from within Deleuze's work, can be found in his work with Guattari in *What is Philosophy?*

According to the Deleuzian approach, each time we come from problem-solving with clean and applicable principles, we blunder into new extensions and complexities and our blunt tools do no good and have unforeseen negative results. For Deleuze, experimentation must seek as great a connection as possible through large metaphysical structures. It is error-prone in a different way to abstraction. Experimentation is necessarily subject to chance, destructiveness and failure in that it has to select individual aesthetic paths through problems that cannot be resolved (*let's try this*) rather than being error-prone through wilful omission (*we have evidence for the value of this principle*).

Due to the priority given to metaphysics and to a view of the individual as a Leibnizian monad twisted through a complex and tense system, science plays a very different role to the one envisaged by Harman. In Deleuze's work, the results of experiments and local theories, such as those of social psychology, are subjected to extended and quite severe critiques of their metaphysical presuppositions: of how the experiments are set up, of what they aim to prove or disprove, of what they consider to be significant or not.[5] His work is more closely attentive to much broader scientific theories as exemplars of the metaphysics, or as counter-theories that need to be taken into account. This attention extends to theories that are very distant from social psychology, such as psychoanalysis and pure mathematics.

Yet, in a surprising reversal, it could also be claimed that Deleuze's work is very close to Harman's good trends. Indeed, in interesting ways, his metaphysics incorporates and is sensitive to them. This closeness is very important in understanding the productive relations that bring Deleuze close to debates in virtue ethics, despite his severe criticisms of Aristotle's metaphysics[6] and his transformation of the notion of value from identifiable values to intensities. Value is not a judgement about a particular quality, characteristic or act (*a valuable thing*). It is a changing level of intensity in a system (*a valuable change to greater intensity or energy*).

It could be said that Deleuze is close to the spirit of what is good according to Harman, but that he objects to the specific characterisation of that goodness. This difference lies in the reasons for entering into the spirit. For Deleuze these reasons are still profoundly metaphysical. They are therefore inimical to a philosophy based on one plane of beliefs, abstract cases and limited empirical science, even though a practice based on them may quite well be important both socially and for an individual life.

In his 'three goods' article, Harman distinguishes special foundationalism from general foundationalism. The former prioritises foundational beliefs over others. It also depends on methods of derivation from foundational beliefs to others: 'Special foundationalists supposed that non-foundational beliefs and methods were justified only if they could be derived from special foundational premises using only foundational methods. The foundational beliefs and methods were foundational in the sense that we must start with them and justify everything else in terms of them.'

This kind of foundationalism is rejected by Deleuze in favour of a dialectical method where all kinds of beliefs enter into a system and where none can claim to be independent of others. Neither can they claim to legislate over them or ground them. However, beliefs have different roles to play in the processes that determine the system.

His transcendental deductions begin with singular and contingent events, then move to broader metaphysical structures, such as transcendental conditions, only to move back to better determined views of the initial events. The transcendental structure is not bottom up, but circular (even this view of circularity is misleading since it remains in a linear view of time. Perhaps the notion of a simultaneous circularity would be better). It is far removed from Kant's transcendental in rejecting pure generalities as starting points for deductions and in arriving at transcendental processes rather than forms of legislation and categories for judgement.

As discussed in the chapter on Deleuze and Kant, this circularity or reciprocal determination raises serious objections regarding the validity of the transcendental deductions and possible objections regarding vicious circles. So, in order to sustain the dialectical movement, no entities or beliefs are finally fixed. Instead, permanence lies in the realms and processes articulating beliefs or entities. For example, the Ideal realm consists of multiplicities of relations between variations that resist final identification. Any individual is determined as a perspective encompassing the Ideal realm according to differing intensities of those relations.

The individual determines a singular set of all relations of the Ideal realm in terms of distinctness and obscurity. There are no absolutely clear relations or things that can claim independence from others. Neither are there any processes relating the Ideas to actual things that can claim to occur free of other processes. Nor are there any actual things independent of the processes and the Ideal realm. Distinctions between beliefs and individuals must be on the basis of relations of intensity, distinct-obscurity, rather than the presence or absence of some other kind of absolutely well-determined evidence (intuitive or deduced).

This means that the derivation and privileging inherent to special foundationalism does not apply to Deleuze's metaphysics. His philosophy is therefore much closer to the general foundationalism advocated by Harman. However, it also means that Deleuze is to be plagued by the two related critical questions that are addressed to virtue ethics: What status can it claim for itself in term of necessity, given its contingent starting points? Is it not prone to contingent inclusions and exclusions dependent on the differences one finds in those points?

Guiding intuitions, curbing subjectivity

Deleuze is not only close to Harman in eschewing special foundationalism and in an interest in practical experiments, though not abstract ones. He is also close in realising that a third term is necessary. Harman completes his anti-foundationalism and advocacy of principles based on intuitive abstractions and reflective equilibrium with an important role for empirical science. He has shown this necessity through arguments on mistaken attribution and a defence of Judith Jarvis Thomson's move to virtuous actions and away from virtuous character.

According to Harman, following John Doris, experiments in contemporary social psychology demonstrate that it is a mistake to infer virtuous character from actions. Given apparently small differences such as time-pressure, character shows itself to be extremely fragile and undependable.[7] We should therefore concentrate our reflection on the virtues on actions rather than character.[8] More importantly, this implies that social structures leading to virtuous actions should take precedence over forms of interaction based on character - kinds of moral education, for example.

Deleuze's philosophy is consistent with this, given its stress on process rather than identity. There could be no such thing as fixed identity, since any individual is always an unsteady and evolving network of processes. However, though the findings of empirical science have a role to play in Deleuze's work, they do not provide the main arguments for the focus on process and the critique of identity.

For example, Deleuze's critique of Aristotle is based around the claim that he has a mistaken definition of being as dependent on analogy. This mistake leads Aristotle's work towards categories and judgements, rather than to a reflection on their becoming. On the one hand, we have the thought that when we say that a thing 'is' we mean that it 'is as an X'. Being then becomes analogical: 'c is an X' *like* 'd is a Y'. On the other hand, we have the thought that 'being is said of all things in the same way'. So 'c' is - *independent of being an 'X'*.

'To be', for Deleuze, means 'to become'. Becoming is seen as more important than being because he defines life as a process of transformation (*How can I live with the way I become different?*) rather than living the best life, as defined by one's category (*What is the best life as an X?*). Famously, in an early address to many of the most important French philosophers of the time, Deleuze caused perplexed rumblings when he claimed that the questions 'Who?' and 'How?' were much more philosophically significant than the question 'What?'[9]

In *Difference and Repetition*, Aristotle's work is seen as governed by the latter question and by reflection on what things are rather than how they have become and what they can become, this brings the work under the yoke of representation, recognition and identity:

> As a concept of reflection, difference testifies to its full submission to all the requirements of representation, which becomes thereby 'organic representation'. In the concept of reflection, mediated and mediating difference is in effect fully subject to the identity of the concept, the opposition of predicates, the analogy of judgement and the resemblance of perception.[10]

Though empirical science can unmask false identities, such as the mistaken attribution of character, it can itself contribute to the emergence of new identities. In this case, the idea that there is an identifiable act and identifiable situations, to take the place of the identifiable character, would itself be open to question.

This does not mean that Deleuze would deny the key point made by John Doris and Stephen Stich in their article 'As a Matter of Fact: Empirical Perspectives on Ethics': 'Philosophical ethics can, and indeed must, interface with the human sciences.[11] Rather, it means that the requirement to take account of the human sciences is but one part of a more complete dialectics, where transcendental conditions and individual sensations and signs are just as important. Science may show that character is not robust, but Deleuze's philosophy seeks to convince us that no determination of identity is metaphysically valid.

There is clearly very great pressure on this notion of metaphysical validity in Deleuze's work. I have developed a reading and defence of Deleuze's metaphysics at length elsewhere. Though, it is important to be aware of the possible weaknesses and errors of his broad arguments, I aimed to respond to more precise objections in this essay. First, is his move away from a central role played by philosophy in moral debate and guidance justified? Second, is it justifiable to focus on individuals and their relation to problems, rather than on shared intuitions, general cases and empirical science?

A summary of Deleuze's answers comes from the following responses. The role of philosophy is to help us to learn how to think and not to dictate what we think.[12] What we think is a necessarily individual matter and only a changeable and secondary part of existence. There are no shared intuitions, general cases or empirical findings that do not require a more complete view in terms of their evolution and in terms of creative responses towards their transformation. To hold to their independent truth is to hold on to a damaging illusion.

Bad trends in philosophy

In defending a move away from common sense and good sense, Deleuze develops a critique of a dominant 'image of thought' that he traces back through the history of philosophy. This image is characterised by eight postulates:

1) to think philosophically presupposes a good will on the part of the thinker;
2) thought is good;
3) there is a common sense that crosses between faculties (recognition)
4) there is a good sense that crosses between thinkers (a shared sense of good and bad, better and worse);
5) recognition depends on representation (identity in the concept, analogy in judgement, oppositions in imagination, similarities in perception);
6) error is a case of false recognition;
7) problems have solutions;

8) knowledge is the goal of learning.

Here is a gloss of Deleuze's responses and objections:

1) all thinkers bring conflicting desires, ideal genealogies and sensa
   tions to thought;
2) thought is always accompanied by a chaotic creative and destructive
   background;
3) faculties evolve through their differences and they cannot be recog
   nised;
4) thinkers cannot divest themselves of their individuating differences
   and good sense is therefore an illusion;
5) the dependence on representation is an illegitimate covering up of
   underlying pure differences and repetitions of those differences;
6) error comes from the struggle of thought with its chaotic background;
7) problems can only be transformed to make an individual life viable;
8) learning is the goal of learning;

The three trends praised by Harman are a return to the postulates that
have failed philosophy. Their goodness is only passing and illusory.

Notes

1) Gilbert Harman, 'Three trends in moral and political philosophy' *http://www.princeton.edu/~harman/Papers/Trends.pdf*

2) By local, I mean opposed to a general and high theoretical type (contemporary cosmology, for example). This is important given the different scientific references in Deleuze and Harman, at least in the context of moral philosophy.

3) This important passage is very difficult to translate and a lot hangs on its translation. The French version is *'Tout corps, toute chose pense et est pensée, pour autant que, reduite à ses raisons intensives, elle exprime une Idée don't elle determine l'actualisation. Mais le penseur lui-même fait de toutes choses ses differences individuelles; c'est en ce sens qu'il est chargé des pierres et des diamants, des plantes "et des animaux meme". Le penseur, sans doute le penseur de l'eternel retour, est l'individu, l'universel individu. Cest lui qui se sert de toute la puissance du clair et du confus, du clair-confus, pour penser L'Idée dans toute sa puissance comme distincte obscure. Aussi faut-il constamment rappeler le charactère multiple, mobile et communiquant de l'individualité: son charactère impliqué.'* (DR 327) I depart from the Patton translation in rendering 'des pierres' (etc.) as 'the stones' rather than stones - in order to reflect that, through the Idea, all stones run through individuals. I prefer to translate 'chargé' as 'charged' rather than burdened - in order to keep its affirmative sense. My translation of individual universal is designed to reflect that Deleuze avoids the French 'L'individu universel' or universal individual in favour of the more strange 'universel individu' that can be translated as universal individual but only at the cost of losing the emphasis on universal and Deleuze's constant claim that the only universal is the individual.

4) See Deleuze's early books on Kant (*Kant's Critical Philosophy*), Bergson (*Bergsonism*) or Hume (*Empiricism and Subjectivity*) for examples of such inclusive and cross-faculty readings.

5) These critiques can be traced back to work on the concept in Deleuze's *Difference and Repetition* (pp 12-14).

6) See my *Gilles Deleuze's Difference and Repetition: a Critical Introduction and Guide* pp 59-63.

7) See John Doris, *Lack of Character: Personality and Moral Behaviour* (Cambridge University Press, 2002)

8) See Gilbert Harman 'Virtue ethics without character traits' *http://www.princeton.edu/~harman/Papers/Thomson.html* and his review of Hursthouse's *On Virtue Ethics*, *http://www.princeton.edu/~harman/Papers/Hursthouse.pdf*

9) See 'La méthode de dramatisation'

10) *Difference and Repetition*, p 35

11) 'As a matter of fact: empirical perspectives on ethics' in Jackson and Smith *Oxford Handbook of Analytic Philosophy*, forthcoming. *http://www.rci.rutgers.edu/%7Estich/Papers_Available_OnLine_Master_File/Matter%20of%20Fact.htm*

12) See, for example, Deleuze's politically engagé articles on the Group Information

Prisons and on Arafat in *L'Île déserte et autres textes* and *Deux regimes de fous* ('"Ce que les prisoniers attendent de nous…"' and 'Grandeur de Yasser Arafat').

8

Deleuze, Negri, Lyotard:
metaphysics and resistance

In the essay 'Kairòs, Alma Venus, Multitudo' in *Time for Revolution*, his account of the ontology underlying *Empire* (one of the most important contemporary books about political resistance and globalisation, co-written with Michael Hardt and deeply influenced by Deleuze), Antonio Negri refers to Pascal's famous 'reed' fragment: 'Man is but a reed, weakest in nature, but he is a thinking reed.' (*Pensées*, fragment 186, Gallimard 1977) In line with the definition of metaphysics as a dynamic structure of relations put forward here, the hierarchy and distinction implied by this passage matter less to Pascal's metaphysics than the processes that underlie them. It is what reason allows man to do - to rise to God - and how that resists the existential crises implied by the hierarchy that is significant for Pascal: 'But when the universe came to crush him, man would still be more noble than what killed him because he would know that he was dying and the universe would know nothing of its advantage.' The universe cannot raise itself; man can. Through reason, man resists death. Negri's point is not to advocate Pascal's turn to God; far from it. His interest is in Pascal's appeal to reason. Like Deleuze, Negri wants to show the resisting power of reason and, more accurately and with greater completeness, of thought allied to desire.

For Negri and for Deleuze, a metaphysics and an ontology describe and set the conditions for resistance. As such, they can either curtail resistance or energise it. This book has tried to show how Deleuze's maximally open metaphysics resists tendencies to close off different forms of life, different creative processes and different experiences. In this conclusion, I want to point to wider consequences of my reading of Deleuze's metaphysics, not in order to give some definitive account of his politics - a task far beyond the scope of my study - but in order to give a sense of the potential and boundaries of his work through a reflection on how resistance is shaped by it. In such terms, my reading has attempted to show how alternative metaphysics to

Deleuze's fail to resist a return to exclusive identities as successfully as his arguments for the reciprocal determination of actual and virtual realms. However, key political questions then come to the fore: Can such openness lay claim to a more practical power of resistance? Is the concept of resistance one that is rendered sharper and more practicable through Deleuze's work? Or does it become a relative term, to the point where it becomes lost in a thicket of subjective and individual positions - prefigured in Deleuze's dependence on the concept of the individual?

In light of such questions, a first challenge to a metaphysics, defined as dynamic and maximally open, comes out of a mistaken definition of resistance. If resistance is defined as resisting movement or change, then all processes where identifiable differences encounter one another are sites of resistance - on all sides. The guard may well be resisting, sitting on a stool, outside the cell of the dying prisoner of conscience. Resistance then becomes a competition between incompatible identities and positions, as they struggle to defend what they have and extend their dominion over others. This is resistance at its most conservative and reactionary, even when it is in the name of progress and relative change. The critical questions then become: How can we ascribe values to different forms of resistance through Deleuze's metaphysics? Can resistance be a functional concept, if it applies everywhere, only varying according to attention and limitations of knowledge or taste? Would it not require an external value, for judgements to be made between different resistances? For example, true resistance could be on the side of the greatest resistance, or it could be in the name of a higher truth to which all things should tend. How can resistance, as 'common sense' understands and values it, be a central concept of a metaphysics where all is relative transformation? How can Deleuze decide between different identities and their competing claims?

The answer from Deleuze's work is that things are not generally relative at all and that resistance is never primarily in the name of an identity against an outside force. On the contrary, the connectedness of his metaphysics and the primacy given to differential movements or transformations over identities provide us with clear counter-principles for resistance, for example, that experimentation beyond boundaries and limits is to be valued over guarding them, or that any identity should be criticised from the point of view of the movements that have had to be concealed in order to represent it as an identity at all. True resistance is when guards and prisoners are transformed beyond their opposed positions; when thought goes beyond the identifications that block their situations. Any such thought must not rest primarily on future identities and stagnant situations. Yet, the new Deleuzian principles are still locally relative, in the sense that they do not apply uniformly and, instead, require different actions according to different individuals and situations. This is because each individual has to counter and to work with a different set of identities and movements, of productively destabilising sensations and creative (and hence also destructive) intensities. This is not a relativism of subjective free-choice or inclination, but one of different situations. Individuals express the complete virtual and actual, but not in the same way. So, when Deleuze speaks of a dialectics and when dialectics serves resistance, it is not as universal. It is as a creativity necessarily tailored to individuals. But it is also as a necessarily connected experimental practice; one that must express relations between individuals - both actual and virtual.

As resistance, thought can only be a practice. In this practice, individuals necessarily work with great overlaps in terms of the identities they have to work through. These identities themselves presuppose a genesis in virtual Ideas and evolutions through them. So long as we retain the Deleuzian senses of sensation and reason, creation and experiment, we can say that individuals must 'calculate' with identified environments, but also, with their emotional significance and its Ideal connections. Relativism ascribed to subjects, to judgements and to tastes is therefore not compatible with his philosophy. On the contrary, his position resembles more closely forms of objectivity about political and social states of affairs (except that these will be processes), about revolutionary ideas (except that these will be associated with virtual genetic movements: Deleuze's transcendental Ideas) and about common sensations (except that these will be resistant to theorisation and systematisation as perceptions - they will be individual, but shared, political feelings, rather than programmed reactions). When Negri describes a resisting multitude in terms of singularities set in movement, in common, by sensations in face of poverty, he is setting out a form of resistance consistent with Deleuze's thought: 'Therefore, in the first place, poverty is given as resistance. There exists no experience of poverty that is not at the same time one of resistance against the repression of the desire to live.' (*Time for Revolution*, 201)

Deleuze's metaphysics is a guiding thread for collective movements of resistance. It unmasks defences of illusory and ill-defined resistance that rest on subjective isolation, the strictly personal, the clan, or the sect; these are based on fixed representations of solid foundations, when in reality there are only more and further extended processes, operating at different degrees through all emergent identities. The terror that sects and nations exercise when faced by difference and change is a reflection of the falsity of their grounds. The movements that determine true resistance cannot be based on the person or on the subject, or on uneasy alliances built around them. Instead, intense and liberating movements are pre-personal and pre-subjective conditions. They work through the signs and the sensations that give each individual its singularity, but only as a transformer of common virtual intensities. Though we are moved by the same sensations, such as the power of love in the face of poverty, as defined by Negri ('From this perspective one can say without doubt that the relation between poverty and love is configured as an eternal return of the power of love to the location of poverty.' (*Time for Revolution*, 210)), that which moves us cannot be conceptualised and is not the basis for a purely intellectual and reflective common resistance. Neither is it a purely private feeling that cannot be shared in principle with others, because the Ideas and intensities expressed in one person's feelings are conditions for any actuality and hence any other person's, but to different degrees. This does not mean that there is no place for social and political observation, commentary and critique. On the contrary, it means that this necessary part of the determination of actual situations requires an extension into the Ideal conditions for action. These are expressed through the sensations that accompany this objectivity and through the desires to change it and the creative acts that are generated by them.

Sadly, but not irredeemably, contemporary political activity is often driven by a different form of resistance and type of feeling than the collective, but individually-nuanced and multiple movements described by Deleuze and Negri. This other form is characterised by the search for absolute foundations for resistance. In its most extreme form, it involves the claim that resistance must always be founded on some kind of *ne plus ultra* (a faith or a belief in an absolute truth or value). For such political and faith-based positions, other forms are corrupt or destined to self-destructive relativism. Their definition of resistance, with its appeal to a form of transcendence of truth or of value, is completely opposed to Deleuze's. It is crucial to guard against the possibility of confusing them, in particular, through mistaken interpretations of his appeal to the virtual. There is no absolute in Deleuze's work and every limit, every culmination, allows for a beyond intricately connected to, and transformed by, that which it is supposed to command and curtail. When Deleuze uses the term absolute, it is as an absolute speed: a movement resistant to identity and representation and not a higher form or source of truth. The contrast with Pascal is stark.

For Pascal, thought is a redemptive (though predetermined) process that stands outside geometric space and duration. He draws up a metaphysics where thinking connects to an eternity that is neither a drive to greater spatial expansion nor a temporal infinity. It matters little how far our estate extends and promises to extend, it matters little whether our lives touch on endlessness, we will remain a fragile reed stretched between two infinities: 'All our dignity consists therefore in thought. We must rise from there and not from a space and duration that we could never fill.' Reason, allied to faith, provides a conduit independent of human freedom between two orders: a fallen state in familiar time allied to a space extending to infinity, and an eternal state with God. Infinity is reeled out and can be travelled along, it is countable and segmented. Whereas eternity transcends that which can be measured; it allows for no internal division or radical distinctions.

Eternity, Pascal's absolute, cannot be a matter of degrees of truth, or of accumulation, since the terror of the two infinities would return with the power of imagination (*Imagine how much more is left. Imagine it all going*) The *Pensées* describe the processes of the conduit and how we have failed it. The rules and orders of reason are absolute and incomparable - only negative passions allow for destructive degrees: 'Through space, the universe comprehends me and swallows me up, as it would a point; through thought, I comprehend it.' Reading Pascal whilst imprisoned, Negri admires this commitment to reason and refers to it when he wishes to show the power of thought in a materialism that maintains an independence from physical laws. The *Pensées* must have been the most demanding prison read, combining ascetic determinism with a vivifying sense of the power of reason in the most crushing situations: 'Here is a man in a cell, not knowing whether his death sentence has been given, with only an hour left to find out, or with just that hour left to get it revoked, if he knows that the sentence has been given. It is against nature to use that hour, not to seek out the sentence, but to play piquet.' (*Pensées*,152) For those who still confuse Deleuze's work with a denial of any identity, it is helpful to recall Deleuze's defence of Negri through a demand for an identifiable accusation against him: '... it is necessary that the accusation possess, in its entirety, a minimum of identifiable consistency' ('Lettre ouverte aux juges de Negri' in *Deux régimes de fous*, p 157). True resistance does not deny the necessity of identity, but its priority; identity is a condition, but one to be minimised and one that must serve the push beyond representation and recognition.

Pascal's commitment to reason is tempered by faith as a necessary companion to reason on the way to God: 'Two excesses. To exclude reason and to admit reason alone.' (172) This tempering and the God/universe distinction is what Negri calls the error of the 'transcendental' in philosophy (according to the definitions used in this book, this should be understood as the error of transcendence). In the transcendent error, being is divided into realms. The division and its sufficient reason determine all metaphysical processes within and between the realms. This subjection of all processes to a prior distinction is characteristic of metaphysics of transcendence as opposed to metaphysics of immanence. It is objectionable, at least for thinkers such as Deleuze and Negri, due to the illegitimate or falsifying limits imposed on processes - in Pascal's case on reason, and on the universe. But can there be resistance without such limits and distinctions, and without appeals to the absolute? In escaping transcendence and its accompanying terrors and impositions of identity, does Deleuze's metaphysics not also renounce resistance? Two brief, but powerful, texts by Jean-François Lyotard sketch an answer.

When Gilles Deleuze died in 1995, Lyotard sent two faxes about his friend to *Le Monde* and to *Le Monde des livres*. These are collected in the posthumous collection *Misère de la philosophie*. The two pieces show a Deleuzian resistance to traditional reactions to death and to their hold over us, for example, through the consolation of an afterlife or an irredeemable grief at a senseless loss of an irrecoverable identity. Following Deleuze (and his readings of Spinoza and of Nietzsche), Lyotard defines passion as a decrease in power and as a disconnection from the eternal return of life-affirming differences. This eternal return is not dependent upon prior identities. Instead, it is an eternal return of affections or becomings in actuality. This is not the eternity of figure or form, but of dynamic process; it is the eternity of variation, rather than the eternity of stasis. Deleuze's work was already a sign for resistance to his own death:

> He was too tough to experience disappointments and resentments - negative affections. In this nihilist *fin de siècle*, he was affirmation. Right through to illness and death. Why did I speak of him in the past? He laughed, he is laughing, he is here. It's your sadness, idiot, he'd say. (Lyotard, *Misère*, 194)

> One cannot act on time, on space, on the world in totality, or define them - they are flat and unstable networks of lines. One has to thread one's way within them, helping lines to meet, which can then be an event, an intensity and carry a name. That the History of the world could be the coming of sense or its decline, made [Deleuze] laugh uncontrollably. The world-historical is the cherished object of power paranoids. Sense is an unexpected flower, a supplement of tension that grows out of an encounter that remains ungraspable for hermeneutics and semiotics. The flower opens without noise. It is an accent, a tone, a strange mode of the voice, of a voice that is neither mine, nor that of things - a figural, he said of Francis Bacon. If you count time with a watch, time passes fast. In his intemporal time, it does

not pass at all. (*Misère*, 196)

In these moving and personal testimonies to a friendship and intellectual union resistance is neither easy, nor indifferent. (The note on the figural in *The Logic of Sensation* was one of the very few times Deleuze quoted Lyotard's work. The concept of the figural is from his *Discours, figure*. It is one of Lyotard's most enduring and beautiful concepts for the event.) Like many of Deleuze's friends, Lyotard remembers his laughter and good humoured resolve. His recollections could then be cause for despair at a passing away - a loss. The memories, though, are put into the context of the resistance to nihilism that runs through Lyotard's late writings on Malraux and Augustine. They are examples of a wider philosophical point. Lyotard contrasts individual sensations, connecting us with others, to a wider nihilism and loss of creative energy and values. Resistance through affects and against negative passions is part of a resistance to indifference and to sameness in wider political and social structures. Laughter is eternal, whereas nostalgia and sadness remain time-bound due to their dependence on historical identifications. Lyotard sees the end of the Twentieth Century as particularly marked by nihilism; in the sense that nihilism was the dominant trend rather than one movement among many. But, Deleuze's work resists this nihilism and its connection to death as loss of identity.

In his letters to *Le Monde*, Lyotard stresses how affirmation as resistance can pass out of historical time, but without having to posit a form of transcendence that would replicate the structure of nihilism (belief in Deleuze's soul, for instance). He therefore moves beyond a time-bound nihilism, to reflect on the wider transforming relation between historical time and eternal return. It is not possible for historical time to remain linear and subject to teleology if it maintains a more truthful relation to the event. Reflecting on Deleuze's metaphysics, Lyotard sees the event as cancelling out claims made for world-historical time in terms of direction and value. There is no such thing as an overall progress or decay (the coming or decline of sense). There is no such thing as a historical logic of events or a final truth of historical times or epochs. The world-historical must be separated from the transformative and resisting power of the event. This is not a transformation in time, but rather it is the way an affirmative affect touches a generative multiplicity that is expressed in different ways in all things and at all times - the challenge for resistance is then to play it anew and with greater intensity.

This event is a-subjective, resistant to objectification and beyond representation: 'neither mine nor of things', 'ungraspable'. It cannot belong to subjects, including an inter-subjectivity. It is not scientific, nor linguistic (in a structural sense as representation; that is, there can be events in language, but language cannot capture events). The event is therefore individual, not in the sense of belonging to an individual, or in any sense of individualism, but in the sense of providing an individual perspective on the world-historical and a movement in it through the eternal return of difference within structures that tend to sameness. The affirmative affect therefore travels through all processes, at greater or lesser degrees, but never completely absent or completely present. It is the disturbance interfering with all others on the surface of a pool. If it did not run through all things, then it would be possible to isolate it, contradicting Lyotard's claims for its power to undermine world-historical sense and for the impossibility of representing it. The event could never be cut off and categorised: 'It remains that in becoming the earth has lost any centre, not only within itself, but also as something to revolve around. Bodies no longer have a centre, except their death when they are exhausted and return to the earth to be dissolved.' (Deleuze, *Cinema 2*, 186) For Deleuze, bodies may become exhausted, but the processes that gave them their transitory energy remain to be affirmed anew, always, but only through new forms of creative resistance.

Bibliography

Works by Gilles Deleuze:

Note: The excellent research source, *webdeleuze.com*, has a comprehensive and carefully prepared Deleuze bibliography by Timothy S. Murphy, *http://www.webdeleuze.com/TXT/ENG/GDBIB2.htm*

Empirisme et subjectivité: essai sur la nature humaine selon Hume (Paris: Press Universitaires de France, 1953). Boundas, C, *Empiricism and Subjectivity: An Essay on Hume's Theory of Human Nature* (New York: Columbia University Press, 1991)

Nietzsche et la philosophie (Paris: Presses universitaires de France, 1962). Trans. Tomlinson, H. *Nietzsche and Philosophy* (New York: Columbia University Press, 1983)

La Philosophie critique de Kant: doctrine des facultés (Paris: Presses universitaires de France, 1963. Trans. Tomlinson, H. and Habberjam, B. *Kant's Critical Philosophy: The Doctrine of the Faculties* (Minneapolis: University of Minnesota Press, 1984)

Le Bergsonisme (Paris: Presses universitaires de France, 1966). Trans. Tomlinson, H. and Habberjam, B. *Bergsonism* (New York: Zone Books, 1990)

"Gilbert Simondon. -- *L'Individu et sa genèse physico-biologique*" (book review) in *Revue philosophique de la France et de l'étranger* CLVI:1-3 (janvier-mars 1966), pp.115-118. Trans. Ramirez, I. 'Review of Gilbert Simondon's *L'Individu et sa genèse physico-biologique* (1966)' Pli, The Warwick Journal of Philosophy, Volume 12, 2001, pp 43-9.

Présentation de Sacher-Masoch (Paris: Éditions de Minuit, 1967). Trans. McNeil, J. *Masochism* (New York: Zone Books 1989).

Différence et répétition (Paris: Presses Universitaires de France, 1968). Trans. Patton, P. *Difference and Repetition* (New York: Columbia University Press, 1994)

Spinoza et le problème de l'expression (Paris: Éditions de Minuit, 1968). Trans. Joughin, M. *Expressionism in Philosophy: Spinoza* (New York: Zone Books, 1990)

Logique du sens (Paris: Éditions de Minuit, 1969). Trans. Lester, M. and Stivale, C. *The Logic of Sense* (New York: Columbia University Press, 1990)

Proust et les signes (Paris: Presses universitaires de France, 1970). Trans. Howard, R. *Proust and Signs* (New York: George Braziller, 1972)

and Félix Guattari *Capitalisme et schizophrénie tome 1: l'Anti-Oedipe* (Paris: Éditions de Minuit, 1972). Trans. Hurley, R., Seem, M. and Lane, H.

Anti-Oedipus: Capitalism and Schizophrenia (New York: Viking Press, 1977) and Félix Guattari: *Kafka: Pour une litterature mineure* (Paris: Éditions de Minuit, 1975). Trans. Polan, D. *Kafka: Toward a Minor Literature* (Minneapolis: University of Minnesota Press, 1986) and Claire Parnet: *Dialogues* (Paris: Flammarion, 1977). Trans. Tomlinson, H. and Habberjam, B. *Dialogues* (New York: Columbia University Press, 1987) and Félix Guattari: *Capitalisme et schizophrénie tome 2: Mille plateaux* (Paris: Éditions de Minuit, 1980). Trans. Massumi, B. *A Thousand Plateaus: Capitalism and Schizophrenia* (Minneapolis: University of Minnesota Press, 1987)

Spinoza: philosophie pratique (Paris: Editions de Minuit, 1981). Trans. Hurley, R. *Spinoza: Practical Philosophy* (San Francisco: City Lights, 1988)

Francis Bacon: Logique de la Sensation (Paris: Éditions de la Différence, 1981). Trans. Smith, D. *Francis Bacon: the Logic of Sensation* (University of Minnesota Press, 2003)

Cinema-1: L'Image-mouvement (Paris: Éditions de Minuit, 1983). Trans. Tomlinson, H. and Habberjam, B. *Cinema 1: The Movement-Image* (Minneapolis: University of Minnesota Press, 1986)

Cinéma-2: L'Image-temps (Paris: Éditions de Minuit, 1985). Trans. Tomlinson, H. and Galeta, R. *Cinema 2: The Time-Image* (Minneapolis: University of Minnesota Press, 1989)

Foucault (Paris: Éditions de Minuit, 1986). Trans. Hand, S. *Foucault* (Minneapolis: University of Minnesota Press, 1988)

Le Pli: Leibniz et le baroque (Paris: Éditions de Minuit, 1988). Trans. Conley, T. *The Fold: Leibniz and the Baroque* (Minneapolis: University of Minnesota Press, 1993)

Pourparlers 1972-1990 (Paris: Éditions de Minuit, 1990). Trans. Joughin, M. *Negotiations 1972-1990* (New York: Columbia University Press, 1995) and Félix Guattari: *Qu'est-ce que la philosophie?* (Paris: Éditions de Minuit, 1991). Translation Tomlinson, H. and Burchell, G. *What is Philosophy?* (New York: Columbia University Press, 1994)

Constantin V. Boundas (Ed.) *The Deleuze Reader* (New York: Columbia University Press, 1993)

Critique et clinique (Paris: Editions de Minuit, 1993). Trans. Smith, D. and Greco, A. *Essays Critical and Clinical* (Minneapolis: University of Minnesota Press, 1997)

Gilles Deleuze (et al) 'Gilles Deleuze' *Philosophie*, numero 47, 1995 (includes the important last essay by Deleuze 'L'Immanence: une vie...'

Gilles Deleuze *L'Île déserte et autres texts, textes et entretiens 1953-1974* (Paris: Minuit, 2002). Trans. M. Taormina *Desert Islands and Other*

163

Texts (New York: Semiotext(e), 2003)

Gilles Deleuze *Deux régimes de fous, textes et entretiens 1975-1995* (Paris: Minuit, 2003).

Gilles Deleuze 'Comment est-ce que je vais sortir de ma sphère des possibles?' Cours, Vincennes, 17/05/1983, at *webdeleuze.com*

Selected Works on Gilles Deleuze:

Alliez, Eric (ed.) *Gilles Deleuze: une vie philosophique* (Paris: PUF, 1998)

Ansell Pearson, Keith (ed.) *Deleuze and Philosophy: the Difference Engineer* (London: Routledge, 1977)

Ansell Pearson, Keith *Germinal Life: The Difference and Repetition of Gilles Deleuze* (London: Routledge, 1999)

Badiou, Alain *Deleuze: La Clameur de l'Etre* (Paris: Hachette, 1997). Trans. Burchill, L. *Deleuze: the Clamour of Being* (Minneapolis: University of Minnesota Press, 2000)

Bogue, Ronald *Deleuze and Guattari* (London: Routledge, 1989)

Buchanan, Ian *Deleuzism: a Metacommentary* (Durham: Duke University Press)

Buchanan, Ian and Colebrook, Claire *Deleuze and Feminist Theory* (Edinburgh University Press, 2000)

Buchanan, Ian and Marks, John *Deleuze and Literature* (Edinburgh University Press, 2001)

Boundas, Constantin and Olkowski, D (eds) *Deleuze and the Theatre of Philosophy* (London: Routledge, 1994)

Colebrook, Claire *Gilles Deleuze* (London: Routledge, 2002)

Colebrook, Claire *Understanding Deleuze* (London: Allen and Unwin, 2003)

DeLanda, Manuel *Intensive Science and Virtual Philosophy* (London: Continuum, 2002)

Goodchild, Philip *Gilles Deleuze and the Question of Philosophy* (London: Associated University Press, 1994)

Goodchild, Philip *Deleuze and Guatarri: an Introduction to the Politics of Desire* (London: Sage, 1996)

Hardt, Michael *Gilles Deleuze: an Apprenticeship in Philosophy* (London: UCL, 1993)

Holland, Eugene *Deleuze and Guattari's Anti-Oedipus: an Introduction to Schizoanalysis* (London: Routledge, 1999)

Howie, Gillian *Deleuze and Spinoza* (Basingstoke: Palgrave, 2002)

Kennedy, Barbara *Deleuze and Cinema* (Edinburgh University Press, 2001)

May, Todd Gilles *Deleuze: a General Introduction* (Cambridge University Press, 2005)

Marks, John *Gilles Deleuze: Vitalism and Multiplicity* (London: Pluto Press, 1998)

Massumi, Brian *A User's guide to Capitalism and Schizophrenia* (Cambridge, MA: MIT, 1992)

Parr, Adrian *The Deleuze Dictionary* (Edinburgh University Press, 2005)

Patton, Paul (ed.) *Deleuze: a Critical Reader* (Oxford: Blackwell, 1996)

Patton, Paul *Deleuze and the Political* (London: Routledge, 2000)

Patton, Paul and Protevi, John (eds.) *Between Deleuze and Derrida* (London: Continuum, 2003)

Protevi, John *Political Physics: Deleuze, Derrida and the Body Politic* (London: Continuum, 2002)

Rajchman, John *The Deleuze Connections* (Cambridge MA: MIT, 2000)

Williams, James 'Deleuze and the Threat of Demonic Nihilism' in Banham and Blake (eds) *Evil Spirits: Nihilism and the Fate of Modernity* (Manchester University Press, 2000)

Williams, James *Gilles Deleuze's Difference and Repetition: a Critical Introduction and Guide* (Edinburgh University Press, 2003)

Zourabichvili, François *Gilles Deleuze: une philosophie de l'événement* (Paris: PUF, 1996)

Other Works Cited:

Bachelard, Gaston *Le nouvel esprit scientifique* (Paris: PUF, 1934)

Bachelard, Gaston *La philosophie du non* (Paris: PUF, 1940)

Bachelard, Gaston *La dialectique de la durée* (Paris: PUF, 1950)

Bachelard, Gaston *La poétique de l'espace* (Paris: PUF, 1957)

Badiou, Alain 'Du cinéma comme emblème démocratique' *Critique*, no 692-693, janvier-février 2005, pp 4-13

Borgès, Jorge 'The Garden of Forking Paths' trans. D. A. Yates, in *Labyrinths* (London: Penguin, 1970) pp 44-54

Borgès, Jorge Luis 'Pierre Menard, Author of the Quixote' in *Labyrinths*, pp 62-71

Dennett, Daniel 'Quining Qualia' in A. Marcel and E. Bisiach, eds. *Consciousness in Modern Science* (Oxford University Press, 1988)

Derrida, Jacques Derrida, 'La mythologie blanche' in *Marges de la philosophie* (Paris: Minuit, 1972) pp 317-18.

Doris, John *Lack of Character: Personality and Moral Behaviour* (Cambridge University Press, 2002)

Doris, John and Stich, Stephen 'As a Matter of Fact: Empirical Perspectives on Ethics' in Jackson and Smith *Oxford Handbook of Analytic Philosophy*, forthcoming.   *http://www.rci.rutgers.edu/%7Estich/Papers_Available_OnLine_Master_File/Matter%20of%20Fact.htm*

Franco, Daniel 'Sur faces: positions du visage chez Levinas et Deleuze' in P. Verstraeten and I. Stengers *Gilles Deleuze* (Paris: Vrin, 1998)

Gatens, Moira 'Through a Spinozist Lens: Ethology, Difference, Power' in Patton (Ed.) *Deleuze: a Critical Reader* (Oxford: Blackwell, 1996)

Gros, Fréderic 'Le Foucault de Deleuze: une fiction métaphysique' in *Philosophie* 47, 1995.

Hardt, Michael and Negri, Antonio *Empire* (Harvard University Press, 2001)

Harman, Gilbert, 'Three Trends in Moral and Political Philosophy' *http://www.princeton.edu/~harman/Papers/Trends.pdf*

Harman, Gilbert 'Virtue Ethics Without Character Traits' *http://www.princeton.edu/~harman/Papers/Thomson.html*

Harman, Gilbert *review of Hursthouse's* On Virtue Ethics, *http://www.princeton.edu/~harman/Papers/Hursthouse.pdf*

Kant, Immanuel *Critique of Pure Reason* (Cambridge University Press, 1999)

Kant, Immanuel *Critique of Judgement* Trans. W. S. Pluhar (Indianapolis: Hackett, 1987)

Kant, Immanuel *Prolegomena to any Future Metaphysics* (Manchester University Press, 1953)

Large, William 'On the Word Other in Levinas', *The Journal for the British Society of Phenomenology*, Volume 27, No 1, Jan. 1996, pp 36-52

Leibniz, Gottfried W. *Philosophical Texts* (Oxford University Press, 1998)

Levinas, Emmanuel *Autrement qu'être ou au delà de l'essence* (La Haye: Martinus Nijhoff, 1974. Trans. Lingis, A. *Otherwise than Being or Beyond Essence* (Dortrecht: Kluwer 1991)

Levinas, Emmanuel *Noms propres* (Paris: Fata Morgana, 1976). Trans. M. Smith, Proper Names (London: Athlone, 1996)

Levinas, Emmanuel, *Totalité et infini: essai sur extériorité* (La Haye: Martinus Nijhoff, 1961). Trans. Lingis, A. *Totality and Infinity: an Essay on Exteriority* (Dortrecht: Kluwer, 1991)

Lewis, David *Counterfactuals* (Oxford: Blackwell, 1973)

Lewis, David *Philosophical Papers, Volume I* (Oxford University Press, 1983)

Lewis, David *On the Plurality of Worlds* (Oxford: Blackwell, 1986)

Lewis, David *Philosophical Papers, Volume II* (Oxford University Press, 1986)

Llewelyn, John *Emmanuel Levinas: the Genealogy of Ethics* (London: Routledge, 1995)

Lyotard, Jean-François *Misère de la philosophie* (Paris: Galilée, 2000)

Negri, Antonio *Time for Revolution* (London: Continuum, 2003)

Pascal, Blaise *Pensées* (Paris: Gallimard, 1977)

Peperzak, Adriaan *To the Other: an Introduction to the Philosophy of Emmanuel Levinas* (West Lafayette: Purdue University Press, 1993)

Proust, Marcel *In Search of Lost Time* (6 volumes) (New York: Modern Library, 1998)

Sartre, Jean-Paul *L'Être et le néant* (Paris: Gallimard, 1943). Trans. H. E. Barnes *Being and Nothingness* (New York: Washington Square Press, 1993)

Simondon, Gilbert *L'Individu et sa genèse physico-biologique* (Paris: PUF, 1964)

Smith, Daniel 'Deleuze and Derrida: Immanence and Transcendence' in P. Patton and J. Protevi (eds.) *Between Derrida and Deleuze* (London: Continuum, 2003)

Spinoza, Baruch *The Ethics and Other Works* (Princeton University Press, 1994)

Stengers, Isabelle *Penser avec Whitehead: une libre et sauvage creation de concepts* (Paris: Seuil, 2002)

Wheeler, Michael *Reconstructing the Cognitive World: the Next Step* (MIT: 2005)

Whitehead, Alfred North *Science and the Modern World* (Cambridge University Press, 1928)

Whitehead, Alfred North 'Immortality' in *The Philosophy of Alfred North Whitehead* ed. P. Schlipp (New York: Tudor, 1941)

Whitehead, Alfred North 'Mathematics and the Good', in *The Philosophy of Alfred North Whitehead*, p 679-80.

Whitehead, Alfred North *Process and Reality* (New York: The Free Press, 1978)

Williams, James *Understanding Poststructuralism* (Chesham: Acumen, 2005)

Wittgenstein, Ludwig *Tractatus Logico-Philosophicus* (London: Routledge, 1961)

index